Quick
CREATIVE
CUISINE

Quick
CREATIVE
CUISINE

Val Collins

DAVID & CHARLES
Newton Abbot   London

Page 2 (*From top*) Chickpea and Sesame Dip; Crudités with Dips –
Guacamole, Garlic and Herb, Taramasalata

British Library Cataloguing in Publication Data
Collins, Val
    Quick creative cuisine.
    1. Food: Time-saving dishes – Recipes
    I. Title
    641.555

ISBN 0–7153–9835–0

Typeset by ABM Typographics Ltd, Hull
and printed in Portugal
by Resopal
for David & Charles plc
Brunel House Newton Abbot Devon

Contents

ACKNOWLEDGEMENTS

I should like to express my gratitude to John Plimmer
for taking the photographs for this book and to Michelle Pearce
for preparing and styling the food so beautifully.

My thanks also to Dittman & Malpas, Havant, and
William Morris, Arundel, for supplying props.

Introduction

This very special book has been written for the busy person whose time available for cooking food is limited. Hectic work schedules and increasing interest in leisure activities mean that time is at a premium as never before, while all the new varieties and never-ending displays of commercially pre-prepared meals and cook-chill dishes are very tempting for those who are short of time. But the enticing recipes in this book are just as quick and easy – and nourishing, too! Over the past few years, the link between good eating and good health has been well established. If you know about the food you buy and learn a few new techniques in combining the foods in different ways, you can produce healthy menus like these which will satisfy the most discerning of palates.

Today, the greater emphasis is on buying and cooking good quality, fresh, more nutritious food, because of public awareness of chemical additives and the presence of potentially harmful bacteria in many processed foods. That is not to say that convenience foods should not be used – far from it! Canned, frozen and cook-chill foods are all ideal standbys in the kitchen and are certainly a boon to busy people. Whether cooking for one, two or more, it is important to aim for a diverse, balanced menu and I make no apology for the fact that some of the recipes contain a little butter and cream. 'Moderation in all things' is my motto for healthy but enjoyable eating.

Busy, creative cooks, and the working man or woman with only a little time to shop and prepare food should try to spend a few moments, now and again, to plan and to shop ahead. It will make all the difference to your eating pattern, enabling you to produce an endless variety of dishes and making convenience cooking a far more enjoyable task. Whether you are choosing recipes to feed yourselves at the end of a hard working day or selecting dishes which may be prepared in advance when entertaining, you will find here a selection from my own catalogue of favourites. I feel sure I shall share with you the pleasure of hearing the sighs of delight from friends when something specially prepared, cooked and attractively served is presented to to them for sampling!

You do not need to be a genius in advanced culinary skills to produce good things to eat. On the contrary, most of all good cooking is about inventiveness and adaptation to new ideas. Just a little flair in the art of presentation can make the most simple of foods look appetising.

None of the ingredients for the recipes is particularly unusual or difficult to buy, as I am aware how annoying it can be if you cannot find a particular item. With the growth of supermarkets and decline in the number of specialist shops, it has become increasingly difficult, in some areas, to purchase 'different' foods. However, the necessary ingredient for success is quality. It is essential to choose the freshest fish and top grade fruits and vegetables.

Speed is of the essence, and short cuts in the maximum use of labour-saving kitchen gadgets and appliances are a must. The microwave can help enormously, here, in defrosting, reheating and cooking, as well as in its ability to melt butter, chocolate and gelatin, to heat sauces and gravies, and to warm dinner rolls for last-minute serving. A good food processor or blender will also cut short those time-consuming chores of chopping, sieving, grating, and puréeing.

This book is a must if you are busy. It will fit into your life-style as the recipes have fitted into mine. The good, fast-food dishes are prepared and cooked with the minimum of effort and time. They are healthy to eat without being cranky and prove that cooking for convenience can be deliciously enjoyable!

A Note on Weights and Measures

Throughout, weights and measures have been given in the following order: metric/imperial/USA equivalent.

APPETISERS

SALAD OF PEARS WITH TARRAGON CREAM DRESSING
Serves 2 or 4

2 ripe pears eg Conference or
  William
few drops of lemon juice
60-90ml/4-6tbsp/5-8tbsp
  double cream (heavy cream)
10-15ml/2-3tsp tarragon vinegar
caster sugar, salt and pepper to
  taste
cherry tomatoes, radicchio and
  tarragon leaves for garnish

The contrasting sweet and savoury flavour of this salad makes it go equally well served with cold chicken, pork or ham as a main course. If tarragon vinegar is not available, use white wine vinegar flavoured with a little chopped tarragon, left to marinate for a day or so before straining and using.

1 • Peel the pears then cut into halves lengthways and remove the cores. Sprinkle with lemon juice. (If the pears are ripe and ready to eat they will not need cooking; otherwise, poach the pear halves over a gentle heat in a little sugar and water syrup until tender.)

2 • Beat the cream and tarragon vinegar together until thick and season with caster sugar, salt and pepper.

3 • Slice each half pear lengthways or crossways then fan out the slices and arrange on a serving plate or individual plates with the radicchio leaves.

4 • Either coat the pears with the tarragon cream or place spoonsful at the side. Garnish with cherry tomatoes and tarragon leaves and serve straight away.

200-225g/7-8oz lean back bacon
  rashers, derinded
175g/6oz young spinach leaves
40g/1¹/2oz pine nuts
1 ripe avocado, sliced
50g/2oz Danish Blue cheese,
  crumbled or diced
1 carrot, grated

for the dressing:
juice ¹/2 lemon
45ml/3tbsp/4tbsp olive oil
good pinch of dry mustard
salt and freshly ground black
  pepper

SPINACH AND AVOCADO SALAD
Serves 4-5

The warmed dressing ingredients really bring out the different flavours in the salad.

1 • Cut the bacon into strips and fry in its own fat until crisp. Leave in the pan to keep warm.

2 • If the spinach leaves are large, tear into pieces and then mix with the remaining salad ingredients in a serving bowl.

3 • Whisk all the dressing ingredients together and add to the bacon in the pan. Heat gently and pour over the salad. Toss well and serve straight away.

TOMATO AND BASIL SORBET
Serves 4

1 • Simmer the tomatoes, celery, basil, onion, sugar and lemon juice in a covered saucepan for about 15 min or until tender. Leave to cool.
2 • Purée the mixture in a food processor or blender then rub through a sieve. Season well with Tabasco – the flavour should be enhanced at this stage.
3 • Turn into a rigid freezer container, cover and freeze until half frozen and slushy – about 2 hr.
4 • Whisk the egg whites with the salt until soft peaks form. Fold a little into the half-frozen mixture then fold in the rest. Cover, seal and freeze again until firm.
5 • Place the sorbet into the refrigerator for about 30 min to soften the mixture before serving.
6 • Arrange the sorbet in scoops on chilled plates or individual dishes. Garnish with basil and serve straight away. Serve with savoury biscuits if liked.

450g/1lb tomatoes, roughly chopped
1 large stick celery, sliced
2 large sprigs basil
1 onion, chopped
30ml/2tbsp/3tbsp sugar
30ml/2tbsp/3tbsp lemon juice
few drops Tabasco
2 egg whites
2 pinches salt
basil leaves to garnish
savoury biscuits for serving, optional

MANGE-TOUT AND MUSHROOM MAYONNAISE
Serves 6

1 • Top and tail the mange-tout and blanch in boiling salted water for 1 min. Drain, rinse under cold running water and dry well. Wipe and slice the mushrooms.
2 • Combine the mayonnaise, yoghurt, parsley and half the chives. Beat well, add seasoning to taste, then cover and leave to stand for a while to allow flavours to blend.
3 • Either arrange the mange-tout and the mushrooms on serving plates with a spoonful of mayonnaise on the top of each, or combine the vegetables with the mayonnaise and divide between the plates.
4 • Garnish with the reserved chives.

225g/8oz mange-tout
175g/6oz champignons, marons or oyster mushrooms
150ml/^{1}/4pt/^{2}/3 cup mayonnaise, low calorie if liked
30ml/2tbsp/3tbsp natural yoghurt
60ml/4tbsp/5tbsp chopped parsley
30ml/2tbsp/3tbsp chopped chives
salt and freshly ground black pepper

Previous page (*Clockwise from top left*) Salad of Pears with Tarragon Cream Dressing; Spinach and Avocado Salad; Tomato and Basil Sorbet; Mange-tout and Mushroom Mayonnaise

LETTUCE SOUP WITH WALNUTS
Serves 4–6

1 medium onion, finely chopped
15-30ml/1-2tbsp/1-3tbsp
  vegetable oil
225g/8oz lettuce leaves, washed
  and finely shredded
425ml/³/4pt/2 cups vegetable
  stock
3-4 leaves mint
salt, pepper and a little sugar to
  taste
425ml/³/4pt/2 cups milk
4 egg yolks, beaten
150ml/¹/4pt/²/3 cup natural
  yoghurt or cream
25-40g/1-1¹/2oz walnuts, finely
  chopped

A delicate flavour with a subtle hint of mint for this summer soup which may be served warm or chilled.

1 ♦ Sauté the onion in the vegetable oil for 3-4 min until soft.
2 ♦ Reserve a little lettuce for garnish, add the remainder to the pan and continue to cook for a few minutes until softened.
3 ♦ Stir in the vegetable stock, mint, seasoning and sugar to taste, bring to the boil then simmer for 5 min. Purée in a blender or food processor and return to the pan.
4 ♦ Blend a little of the milk with the egg yolks, stir in the rest. Add to the soup in the pan, and stirring all the time, cook gently until thickened.
5 ♦ Stir in the yoghurt or cream, adjust the seasoning and serve sprinkled with the chopped walnuts and garnished with the reserved shreds of lettuce.

60ml/4tbsp/5tbsp olive oil
1 onion, roughly chopped
275-350g/10-12oz tomatoes,
  roughly chopped
1-2 cloves garlic, crushed or finely
  chopped
275ml/¹/2pt/1¹/4 cups vegetable
  stock
10ml/2tsp tomato purée
salt and freshly ground black
  pepper
10ml/2tsp white wine vinegar
50g/2oz fresh white or
  wholewheat breadcrumbs
275ml/¹/2pt/1¹/4 cups chilled
  vegetable stock or water
selection of chopped onion, diced
  cucumber, peppers, tomatoes
  and croûtons for garnish

CHILLED TOMATO SOUP WITH GARNISHES
Serves 2–3

This is a simpler form of gazpacho.

1 ♦ Heat half the olive oil in a pan and sauté the onion until soft. Add the tomatoes, garlic, stock, tomato purée and seasoning and cook for a further 15-20 min until the vegetables are tender.
2 ♦ Meanwhile, mix the rest of the olive oil with the wine vinegar, toss in the breadcrumbs and leave to soak.
3 ♦ Rub the soup through a sieve, or purée in a food processor or blender then sieve to remove the seeds and the skins of the tomatoes.
4 ♦ Leave to cool before adding the soaked breadcrumbs and chilled stock. Adjust seasoning and serve chilled with the prepared garnishes.

(*From top*) Chilled Tomato Soup with Garnishes; Lettuce Soup with Walnuts

CHESTNUT SOUP
Serves 4–6

25g/1oz butter
1 onion, chopped
1 stick celery, chopped
350g/12oz chestnut purée
1 litre/2pt chicken stock
seasoning
125ml/¹/4pt/²/3 cup single cream
  (light cream)
chopped parsley

1 • Melt the butter, add the onions and celery, fry until soft.
2 • Blend in the chestnut purée and stock. Bring to the boil and simmer, covered, for 15-20 min.
3 • Blend in a processor or pass through a sieve. Return the soup to the pan, season, and warm through.
4 • Add the cream and chopped parsley and serve hot.

HOT SEAFOOD DIP
Serves 6–8

225g/8oz crab meat, fresh,
  canned or frozen, thawed
175g/6oz peeled prawns
2x400g/14oz cans lobster
  or prawn bisque
15ml/1tbsp chopped basil or
  parsley
salt and freshly ground black
  pepper

1 • Flake the crab meat and chop the peeled prawns.
2 • Mix together with the lobster or prawn bisque, herbs and seasoning in a saucepan.
3 • Cook over a gentle heat, stirring until hot through.
4 • Serve hot with bite-sized chunks of french bread for dipping.

CHICKPEA AND SESAME DIP
Serves 4-5

1 x 415g/14¹/2oz can chickpeas
juice 1-2 lemons
45ml/3tbsp/4tbsp tahina
2-3 cloves garlic, crushed
salt
15ml/1tbsp olive oil, optional
5ml/1tsp paprika, optional
5ml/1tsp chopped parsley and a
  few black olives for garnish
warm pitta bread for serving

Hummus is widely available but home-made is easily prepared in a food processor and the ingredients can be adjusted to taste – add a little more garlic, lemon or tahina, for example (photograph page 2).

1 • Drain the chickpeas and reserve the liquid.
2 • Process the chickpeas in a blender or food processor with lemon juice to taste, tahina, garlic and salt and enough of the reserved liquid to obtain a soft creamy consistency.
3 • Serve in individual bowls or on flat plates. Mix the olive oil with the paprika and swirl over the surface of each one if liked. Garnish with a little chopped parsley and a black olive or two. Serve with warm pitta bread for dipping.

CRUDITÉS WITH DIPS
Serves 4–6

A selection of fresh vegetables with one or more of the dips below (photograph page 2).

Prepare the vegetables into bite-size pieces, arrange on a serving platter and keep chilled. Prepare the dips, place into bowls and serve with the vegetables.

red, yellow and/or green pappers
carrots
celery
mushrooms
cauliflower
cucumber
spring onions
fennel

TARAMASALATA DIP

Combine the taramasalata and yoghurt and mix together until smooth. Stir in a few drops Tabasco and Worcestershire sauce to taste.

100-175g/4-6oz taramasalata
75-100g/3-4oz thick Greek yoghurt
Tabasco and Worcestershire sauce to taste

GARLIC AND HERB DIP

Mix the garlic, mayonnaise and soured cream until smooth then stir in the herbs.

2-3 cloves garlic or to taste, crushed
100-150ml/4-5fl oz/^{1}/2-^{2}/3 cup mayonnaise
150ml/^{1}/4pt/^{2}/3 cup soured cream or fromage frais
15-30ml/1-2tbsp/1-3tbsp chopped fresh mixed herbs

GUACAMOLE

Halve, peel and stone the avocados and mash the flesh in a bowl with the lemon juice. Stir in the remaining ingredients and beat until smooth.

2 ripe avocado pears
juice ^{1}/2 lemon
2 tomatoes, skinned, deseeded and chopped
^{1}/2 small onion, grated
1 clove garlic, crushed
few drops Tabasco sauce, to taste
60ml/2tbsp/3tbsp natural yoghurt
salt and freshly ground black pepper

ARTICHOKE AND FENNEL SOUP
Serves 4–6

225g/8oz Jerusalem artichokes
1 bulb fennel
15g/¹/2oz butter
1 onion, roughly chopped
825ml/1¹/2pt/3³/4 cups chicken
  or ham stock or water
5ml/1tsp fennel seeds, crushed
  and pounded
salt and freshly ground black
  pepper
about 150ml/¹/4pt/²/3 cup single
  cream (light cream), to taste
fennel fronds or a few seeds for
  garnish
cheese and peanut scones
  (below) for serving, optional

Delicate flavours of Jerusalem artichoke and fennel blend to make an unusual but delicious country soup.

1 ♦ Peel and slice the artichokes; finely slice the fennel, reserving the fennel fronds for garnish later.
2 ♦ Melt the butter in a saucepan and gently sauté the onion until tender. Stir in the artichokes and fennel and cook for about 5 min until beginning to soften.
3 ♦ Add the stock or water, fennel seeds and seasoning. Bring to the boil then cover and simmer for about 20-25 min until tender, stirring occasionally.
4 ♦ Purée the soup in a food processor or blender and stir in the cream to taste, reserving a little for garnish. Adjust the seasoning and reheat to serve.
5 ♦ Swirl in the remaining cream and garnish with the fennel fronds or seeds. Serve with cheese and peanut scones if liked.

CHEESE AND PEANUT SCONES
Makes about 18

225g/8oz self-raising flour
  (all-purpose flour with double-
  acting baking powder)
pinch salt
40g/1¹/2oz butter
1.25ml/¹/4tsp dry mustard
50-75g/2-3oz Cheddar cheese,
  finely grated
100ml/4fl oz/¹/2 cup milk,
  approximately
50g/2oz unsalted peanuts,
  chopped

These scones are delicious when served warm, straight from the oven, then split and spread with butter. Try a mixture of half white and half wholemeal (wholewheat) flour for a nutty texture.

1 ♦ Preheat the oven to 210°C/gas 7. Sift the flour and salt into a bowl. Cut the butter into small pieces and rub into the flour until it resembles fine breadcrumbs.
2 ♦ Stir in the mustard and grated cheese then add sufficient milk to mix to a soft manageable dough. Knead lightly.
3 ♦ Roll out to about 2cm/³/4in thick and cut into rounds with a 5cm/2in plain cutter and place on to greased baking trays.
4 ♦ Brush the tops with milk and sprinkle with the peanuts. Bake in the preheated oven for about 10 min. Serve warm with butter.

(From top) Cheese Soup with Celery and Smoky Bacon; Lightly Spiced Chicken Soup with Apple and Parsnip; Artichoke and Fennel Soup with Cheese and Peanut Scones

LIGHTLY SPICED CHICKEN SOUP WITH APPLE AND PARSNIP
Serves 4–6

1 large onion
25-40g/1-1¹/2oz butter
100g/4oz peeled parsnip
10ml/2tsp ground cumin
10ml/2tsp mild curry powder or
 paste
30ml/2tbsp/3tbsp flour
425ml/³/4pt/2 cups pure
 unsweetened apple juice
650ml/1¹/4pt/3 cups rich chicken
 stock
150-175g/5-6oz scraps cooked
 chicken meat
225-275g/8-10oz dessert apples
salt and pepper

This recipe provides a good way of using cooked chicken and the combination of spices, apples and parsnips gives a wonderful flavour.

1 • Gently sauté the onion in a little of the butter for about 15 min until tender.
2 • Meanwhile, cut the parsnip into 6mm/¹/4in dice and place into fast boiling water, bring back to the boil quickly then drain and dry well.
3 • Stir the cumin and curry powder or paste into the onion and cook for a minute. Add the flour and stir again.
4 • Pour on the liquids and add the chicken to the pan. Bring to the boil, stirring, then cover and simmer for 10 min until the onion is very tender.
5 • Meanwhile, peel and dice the apples and sauté them in a frying-pan with the parsnips, in a little more of the butter, for 5 min or so until lightly golden.
6 • Add the contents of the frying-pan to the soup, adjust seasoning and serve.

AVOCADO AND YOGHURT SOUP
Serves 3–4

15ml/1tbsp oil
1 small onion, finely chopped
2 medium-size avocados, thinly
 sliced
salt and freshly ground black
 pepper
pinch nutmeg and extra for
 sprinkling
275-425ml/¹/2-³/4pt/1¹/4-2
 cups milk
275ml/¹/2pt/1¹/4 cups natural
 yoghurt

A gentle infusion of flavours provides an elegant summer soup which may be served hot or chilled.

1 • Heat the oil in a pan and sauté the onion until soft.
2 • Save a few slices of avocado for garnish and add the rest to the onion with seasoning and nutmeg to taste.
3 • Add 275ml/¹/2pt/1¹/4 cups of the milk to the pan and heat through gently to allow the flavours to infuse, then purée in a food processor or blender.
4 • Stir in the yoghurt and add more milk to achieve the desired consistency. Adjust the seasoning and heat again if required.
5 • Serve hot or chilled, garnished with the reserved slices of avocado and sprinkled with a little nutmeg.

CHEESE SOUP WITH CELERY AND SMOKY BACON
Serves 2–3

This recipe can be used as a base for almost any cheese soup. It is a good way to use up last pieces of Stilton, while Red Leicester or Double Gloucester give a good colour to the soup.

1 • Melt the butter in a saucepan and gently sauté the onion and celery until soft.
2 • Stir in the flour and, away from the heat, gradually stir in the milk and stock.
3 • Slowly bring to the boil, stirring all the time until the soup has thickened, then reduce the heat and simmer gently for 10 min.
4 • Save a little of the cheese for garnish; then whisk the rest into the soup with salt and pepper to taste. Add a little extra milk if required to thin the soup to your liking.
5 • Grill the bacon until crisp and crumble. Sprinkle over the top of the soup with the remaining cheese before serving.

25g/1oz butter
1 small onion, finely chopped
1 stick celery, finely sliced
25g/1oz flour
275ml/1/2pt/11/4 cups milk, approximately
275ml/1/2pt/11/4 cups chicken or vegetable stock
75-100g/3-4oz cheese, grated
salt and freshly ground black pepper
2-3 rashers lean smoked bacon, derinded

CHILLED MELON SOUP
Serves 4

1 • Halve the melon and scoop out the seeds. Remove the peel from the flesh using a sharp knife.
2 • Cut the flesh into small cubes, then process in a blender or food processor with the sugar until smooth.
3 • Whisk in the wine, yoghurt and lemon juice if liked and chill. Serve garnished with mint leaves.

1 small ripe melon, such as Ogen, Galia or Charantais
15ml/1tbsp caster sugar
100ml/4fl oz dry white wine
150ml/1/4pt/2/3 cup natural yoghurt
juice 1/2 lemon, optional
mint leaves to garnish

SMOKED TROUT PÂTÉ
Serves 6

3 smoked trout, skinned and boned
juice 1 lemon
1.25ml/^{1}/4tsp cayenne
ground black pepper
75g/3oz cream cheese
15g/^{1}/2oz butter, melted
75g/3oz smoked salmon, cut into
  6mm/^{1}/4in strips
lemon or lime slices for garnish
sesame toasts for serving

1 ♦ Flake the fish and mash together with the lemon juice, cayenne and black pepper to taste. Blend until smooth.
2 ♦ Cream the cheese lightly, add to the fish with the melted butter and mix well. Alternatively, purée together in a blender or food processor.
3 ♦ Press the mixture into a pudding basin and chill until firm.
4 ♦ Turn out on to a serving plate and garnish the mound of pâté with strips of smoked salmon in a lattice style and lemon or lime slices. Serve with sesame toasts.

SESAME TOASTS

thin slices of French baguette
butter
sesame seeds

1 ♦ Toast the bread on one side under a hot grill.
2 ♦ Butter the untoasted side and sprinkle with sesame seeds.
3 ♦ Grill the untoasted side until golden brown. Serve warm.

HAZELNUT PÂTÉ
Serves 5–6

15-30ml/1-2tbsp/1-3tbsp
  vegetable oil
100g/4oz mushrooms, finely
  chopped
1 clove garlic, crushed
225g/8oz hazelnuts, ground in a
  food processor or blender
salt and freshly ground black
  pepper
2.5ml/^{1}/2tsp grated nutmeg
50-75g/2-3oz cream or curd
  cheese, to taste
15-30ml/1-2tbsp/1-3tbsp
  tomato purée, to taste
few herbs or slice of orange or
  lemon for garnish
fingers of toast for serving

The ground hazelnuts give a crunchy texture to this pâté.

1 ♦ Heat the oil and gently sauté the mushrooms and garlic for a few minutes until tender. Drain well and reserve the juices.
2 ♦ Stir in the ground hazelnuts, seasoning and nutmeg and mix well. Then add sufficient cream or curd cheese and tomato purée to taste.
3 ♦ Add a few drops of the reserved juices to the mixture if necessary to give a soft consistency, and adjust the seasoning.
4 ♦ Divide the pâté between 4 individual ramekin dishes. Garnish with a few herbs or a twist of orange or lemon before serving with fingers of toast.

(*From top*) Smoked Trout Pâté with Sesame Toasts; Pâté de Foie Gras with Quails' Eggs; Cheese and Herb Pâté with Toasted Bread Case; Hazelnut Pâté

PÂTÉ DE FOIE GRAS WITH QUAILS' EGGS
Serves 6

225/8oz pâté de foie gras
6 quails' eggs, hard-boiled and
  halved
24 stoneless black or green olives
295g/10¹/2oz can beef consommé
10ml/2tsp gelatin
chopped parsley for garnish

This is so easy to prepare but very effective for a dinner party.

1 • Divide the pâté into 6 and spread each piece over the base and sides of 6 individual small dishes or ramekins. Nestle half a cold shelled quail's egg with the cut side downwards into each one and surround it with 4 olives.
2 • Place 45ml/3tbsp/4tbsp consommé into a small pan and sprinkle on the gelatin. Stir lightly and heat gently until the gelatin is dissolved.
3 • Add the rest of the consommé to the gelatin and spoon it over the pâtés. Nestle half a quail's egg with the cut side upwards into the centre of each one. Chill for 1 hr in the refrigerator or until set.
4 • Garnish each one with parsley before serving cold.

CHEESE AND HERB PÂTÉ
Serves 4

225g/8oz cream cheese
1 egg yolk
1-2 cloves garlic, crushed
salt
30ml/2tbsp/3tbsp fresh chopped
  herbs
50g/2oz butter, softened
fingers toast or toasted bread cases
  for serving
mint leaves for garnish, optional

1 • Beat together the cheese, egg yolk, garlic and a little salt. Fold in the herbs and stir in the butter. Leave to harden in the refrigerator.
2 • Spoon into a piping bag with a large fluted nozzle. Swirl on to plates and serve with fingers of toast, or pipe into the toasted bread cases. Garnish with mint if liked.

TOASTED BREAD CASES
Makes 4

4 large slices bread, cut
  2.5-4cm/1-1¹/2in thick
40-50g/1¹/2-2oz butter, melted

1 • Cut rounds from the bread slices using a 9-10cm/3¹/2-4in cutter. Cut a circle from inside the round using a cutter 1.25cm/¹/2in smaller, cutting down to within about 1cm/¹/3in from the base.
2 • Insert a knife into the side of the bread round at 1cm/¹/3in above the base, and cutting horizontally and swivelling the knife, cut away and remove the centre section.
3 • Brush the bread cases liberally inside and out with the melted butter. Bake in a preheated oven at 180°C/gas 4 for about 20 min until golden brown.

MONKFISH PÂTÉ
Serves 3–4

1 ◆ Wash the fish and place in a saucepan.
2 ◆ Squeeze the juice from ½ the lemon, chop the flesh of the other ½ lemon and add to the fish. Cover and simmer gently until tender. Drain off the liquid.
3 ◆ Beat the eggs together with the tomato purée and seasoning. Chop the monkfish into small pieces.
4 ◆ Mix the monkfish with the tomato and egg mixture and pour into individual ramekins. Cover with foil, place in a roasting tin of water and bake at 170°C/gas 3 for 30-40 min.
5 ◆ Cool the pâtés and then chill.
6 ◆ Garnish with tomato. Serve with mayonnaise and toast fingers.

350g/12oz monkfish
1 lemon
15g/¹/₂oz butter
2 eggs
65g/2¹/₂oz tomato purée
seasoning
tomato slices for garnish

KIPPER PÂTÉ
Serves 4–6

1 ◆ Grill the kippers 5-10 min, according to size, if fresh, or follow instructions on the packet if frozen. Skin the fillets and allow to cool.
2 ◆ Blend or process until fine. Add cheese and flavourings and blend until well mixed.
3 ◆ Place in a container and chill in refrigerator.
4 ◆ Garnish with parsley and serve with fingers of hot toast.

225g/8oz kipper fillets, fresh or frozen
225g/8oz cream cheese
5ml/1tsp lemon juice
few drops tabasco sauce
pinch white pepper

SLICED CUCUMBER AND AVOCADO WITH CORIANDER
Serves 6

1 ◆ Arrange the cucumber overlapping around the edge of individual serving plates.
2 ◆ Halve, stone and peel the avocados. Slice thinly lengthways, then fan out and arrange in the centres of the cucumber slices.
3 ◆ Whisk the coriander seeds into the french dressing and brush over the cucumber and avocados. Garnish each plate with fresh coriander or parsley.

1 cucumber, very thinly sliced
3 ripe avocados
2.5ml/¹/₂tsp coriander seeds, crushed
75-90ml/5-6tbsp/6-7tbsp french dressing (page 40)
fresh coriander or parsley for garnish

FRIKADELLER
Serves 4

After cooking, these little deep-fried pork balls can be threaded on to skewers for serving if preferred.

1 ‣ Mince (grind) the meat and onion twice or chop finely in a food processor. Mix with the seasoning, flour and egg.
2 ‣ Add sufficient single cream (light cream) or milk to give a mixture which is soft but will hold its own shape.
3 ‣ Use two spoons to divide and shape the mixture into about 24 small balls.
4 ‣ Heat the oil until it will brown a cube of bread in 1 min then fry the frikadeller, in two batches if necessary, until golden brown.
5 ‣ Drain on kitchen paper (paper towels) and thread on to skewers if liked. Serve with tomato sauce and garnish with oregano.

450g/1lb lean pork, cubed
1 small onion
salt and freshly ground black pepper
30ml/2tbsp/3tbsp plain flour (all-purpose flour)
1 egg, beaten
single cream (light cream) or milk
oil for deep-frying
tomato sauce for serving (below)
oregano leaves for garnish, optional

TOMATO SAUCE

This tomato sauce can also be used as a base filling for pizzas, or tossed with cooked pasta and served sprinkled liberally with freshly grated Parmesan cheese.

1 ‣ Gently sauté the onion in the olive oil in a saucepan with the garlic until soft.
2 ‣ Add the rest of the ingredients, cover and simmer for 15 min or until the tomatoes are tender. Then if necessary, simmer briskly for a few minutes to reduce the liquid and thicken the sauce.
3 ‣ Serve the sauce as it is or purée in a food processor and rub through a sieve to remove the pips.
4 ‣ Adjust the seasoning and serve hot or cold.

1 medium onion, finely chopped
30ml/2tbsp/3tbsp olive oil
1-2 cloves garlic, finely chopped
350g/12oz ripe tomatoes, skinned and roughly chopped (or 1 x 397g/14oz can chopped tomatoes)
salt and freshly ground black pepper
2.5ml/1/2tsp caster sugar
15ml/1tbsp tomato purée
15ml/1tbsp chopped basil or oregano

(From top) Frikadeller with Tomato Sauce; Herring Salad with Beetroot and Apple

HERRING SALAD WITH BEETROOT AND APPLE
Serves 2–3

2 small boiled beetroots, sliced
15ml/1tbsp walnut oil
5ml/1tsp raspberry vinegar
mixed salad leaves or watercress
1 mild red or Spanish onion, sliced
1 apple
4-6 sweet pickled herrings or
  rollmops
40g/1¹/₂oz walnuts, optional
soured cream and black rye bread
  and butter for serving

A quickly prepared and unusual way to serve pickled herrings.

1 • Coat the beetroot slices with oil and vinegar and lay on a shallow serving dish with salad or watercress.
2 • Push the onion slices into rings and arrange in the dish.
3 • Cut the unpeeled apple into crescent slices and coat with oil and vinegar to prevent discoloration, and add to serving dish.
4 • Top with the herrings and garnish with the walnuts if liked.
5 • Serve with bowl of soured cream and black rye bread and butter.

MEDITERRANEAN FISH SOUP
Serves 4–6

350g/12oz each of grey mullet,
  whiting and plaice
90ml/6tbsp/7tbsp olive oil
1 large onion, finely chopped
1 clove garlic, crushed
400-450g/14-16oz can
  tomatoes
30ml/2tbsp/3tbsp tomato purée
15ml/1tbsp chopped parsley
825ml/1¹/₂pt/3³/₄ cups fish
  stock or water
150ml/¹/₄pt/²/₃ cup dry white
  wine
bay leaf
large piece of lemon peel
seasoning
150ml/¹/₄pt/²/₃ cup double
  cream (heavy cream)
6 large prawns, peeled
tomatoes, skinned and sliced

1 • Clean, fillet and skin the fish. Cut fillets diagonally into 5cm/2in pieces. The trimmings and bones may be used for stock.
2 • Heat the oil in a large pan. Fry the onion until soft, add the garlic and fry for 1-2 min.
3 • Add the tomatoes, tomato purée and parsley. Mix together and simmer for 5 min.
4 • Add the fish, stock, wine, bay leaf and lemon peel. Cover and continue to simmer for a further 20 min.
5 • Remove bay leaf and lemon peel, also one piece of fish for each serving and keep warm. Season soup and cool slightly.
6 • Pass the soup through a sieve, blender or food processor until blended to a smooth creamy consistency.
7 • Stir in the cream, reheat without boiling.
8 • Place one piece of fish in each individual bowl, pour over soup. Garnish with prawns and slices of tomato.

Note Haddock may be substituted if grey mullet, whiting or plaice are unavailable.

DILL MARINATED MACKEREL WITH MUSTARD SAUCE
Serves 4

1 • Mix together the sugar, salt and ground pepper and sprinkle over both sides of each mackerel fillet, then sprinkle with some of the chopped dill.
2 • Arrange sprigs of dill in the bottom of a dish just large enough to take the fish. Lay the fillets on the dill head to tail, so that they fill the dish evenly. Cover them with the remaining chopped dill.
3 • Cover the fish with plastic film then press lightly with a weight, for example cover with a board and place a 450g/1lb weight on the top. Leave to marinate in the fridge for at least 12 hr.
4 • To serve, scrape off the seasonings and dill from the fillets and cut in very thin slices with a sharp knife, starting at the tail end.
5 • Garnish with dill leaves and serve with lemon wedges, thinly cut rye bread and mustard sauce.

15ml/1tbsp sugar
30ml/2tbsp/3tbsp salt
ground white pepper
4 mackerel, boned and filleted
45-60ml/3-4tbsp/4-5tbsp chopped dill leaves
sprigs dill and extra for garnish
lemon wedges, rye bread and mustard sauce for serving

MUSTARD SAUCE

Combine all the ingredients together and whisk vigorously until thick.

30ml/2tbsp/3tbsp French mustard
10ml/2tsp sugar
15ml/1tbsp white wine vinegar
60ml/4tbsp/5tbsp olive oil
chopped dill leaves to taste
clove garlic, crushed, optional

SCALLOPS GRATINÉES
Serves 4

1 • If the scallops are in the shells, remove them, wash and keep the shells. Rinse scallops in cold water and place in a saucepan. Add water and wine, bring to the boil and simmer for 8-10 min.
2 • Meanwhile fry onion and mushrooms in oil until soft.
3 • Drain off excess oil and mix parsley and seasoning with the mushrooms and onion.
4 • Place a spoonful of this mixture into the 4 shells or individual dishes.
5 • Place two drained scallops in each dish and cover with the remaining mushroom mixture.
6 • Sprinkle with breadcrumbs and dot with butter. Place under a hot grill to crisp the crumbs.

8 scallops
150ml/1/4pt/2/3 cup water
150ml/1/4pt/2/3 cup white wine
1 small onion, chopped
225g/8oz mushrooms, chopped
30ml/2tbsp/3tbsp oil
15ml/1tbsp chopped parsley
seasoning
fresh breadcrumbs
butter

for the marinade:
100ml/4fl oz/1/2 cup cider
  vinegar
100ml/4fl oz/1/2 cup water
45ml/3tbsp/4tbsp caster sugar
1 small onion, chopped
2 small bay leaves
good pinch each white pepper and
  ground allspice

for the herrings:
2 fresh large herrings, boned and
  filleted
275-425ml/1/2-3/4pt/11/4-2
  cups soured cream, to taste
1 medium size onion, quartered
  and thinly sliced
60ml/4tbsp/5tbsp finely sliced
  spring onions, green part only
salt and freshly ground black
  pepper
finely sliced chives for garnish

HERRING FILLETS IN SOURED CREAM
Serves 4–6

Ask the fishmonger to fillet and bone the herrings for you. Any remaining small bones will soften in the marinade.

1 • Combine all the ingredients for the marinade in a pan and bring to the boil. Simmer for 1 min, remove from the heat and leave until cool.
2 • Cut the herring fillets into 2.5cm/1in pieces and arrange in a dish. Pour over the marinade, cover the dish and leave to marinate in the fridge for at least 6 hr.
3 • Remove the herring pieces from the marinade and dry on kitchen paper (paper towels).
4 • Mix together the cream, onions and seasoning and gently stir in the herring pieces. Adjust the seasoning and serve garnished with chives.

225g/8oz smoked salmon
1 ripe avocado
5-10ml/1-2tsp lemon juice
50g/2oz cream cheese
150ml/1/4pt/2/3 cup double
  cream (heavy cream), whipped
freshly ground black pepper
few drops Worcestershire sauce
20ml/4tsp soured cream and a
  little lumpfish roe, optional, for
  garnish
sprigs fresh dill for garnish
fingers brown bread and butter for
  serving

SMOKED SALMON TIMBALES
Serves 4

Try different fillings for the timbales – Smoked Trout Pâté (page 22) or Crab Mousse (page 33) are good alternatives.

1 • Line 4 small ramekin dishes with the slices of smoked salmon, leaving some to allow a lid for each one.
2 • Purée or mash the avocado and mix in the lemon juice and cream cheese. Stir in the whipped cream and add black pepper and Worcestershire sauce to taste.
3 • Divide the mixture between the dishes and top with a lid. Chill until firm.
4 • Turn the timbales out of the dishes on to the serving plates. Top each one with a spoonful of soured cream and a little lumpfish roe. Garnish with sprigs of dill and serve with fingers of brown bread and butter.

(*From top*) Dill-Marinated Mackerel with Mustard Sauce; Smoked Salmon Timbales; Herring Fillets in Soured Cream

CURRIED PRAWN SALAD WITH CAULIFLOWER
Serves 4

1 small cauliflower, cut into tiny
  florets
225g/8oz peeled prawns
60-90ml/4-6tbsp/5-8tbs
  mayonnaise
200-225ml/7-8fl oz/⁷/8-1 cup
  natural yoghurt
2.5ml/¹/2tsp garam masala
¹/2-1 green chilli to taste
4 spring onions, finely sliced
mixed salad leaves for serving
extra prawns and spring onions for
  garnish

*The cauliflower florets provide a crunchy texture to this
mildly spiced salad.*

1 ⋅ Use the cauliflower uncooked for the crispiest texture but, if
preferred, blanch the cauliflower florets for 3-4 min in boiling
salted water then drain and rinse in cold water and dry. Add the
prawns to the cauliflower.
2 ⋅ Mix the quantities of mayonnaise and yoghurt to your taste, but
to give about 275ml/¹/2pt/1¹/4 cups of sauce in total. Blend in the
garam masala and stir in the chilli and spring onions.
3 ⋅ Combine the sauce with the cauliflower and prawns and pile on
to the mixed salad leaves. Garnish with a few extra prawns and
spring onions before serving.

DUCK AND CHESTNUT MOUSSE
Serves 6–8

1 small onion, finely chopped
15g/¹/2oz butter
1 x 425g/15oz can chestnut purée
225g/8oz cooked duck meat
150ml/¹/4pt/²/3 cup double
  cream (heavy cream)
30ml/2tbsp/3tbsp mayonnaise
pinch nutmeg
salt and freshly ground black
  pepper
150ml/¹/4pt/²/3 cup dry white
  wine or stock
1 envelope gelatin
watercress for garnish

*Duck meat and purée of chestnuts are combined to make a rich
and impressive starter.*

1 ⋅ Sauté the onion in the butter until tender. Stir in the chestnut
purée and break down with a wooden spoon.
2 ⋅ Purée the mixture in a food processor or blender or put through a
mincer (grinder) with the duck meat. Mix in the cream, mayonnaise, nutmeg and seasoning.
3 ⋅ Sprinkle the wine or stock with the gelatin in a small pan and
heat gently until the gelatin has softened and dissolved.
4 ⋅ Stir the gelatin mixture into the mousse and pour into a
17.5cm/7in ring mould or similar dish. Chill until firm.
5 ⋅ Turn out on to a serving plate and garnish with watercress. Serve
with thinly sliced toast or sesame toasts (page 22).

DEEP FRIED CAMEMBERT WITH GOOSEBERRY SAUCE
Serves 4

This can be prepared in advance up to method 4, then chilled until required. Deep-fry and serve straight away.

1 ♦ Cut the Camembert into 8 portions and chill for 15-20 min in the freezer.
2 ♦ Prepare the sauce: simmer the gooseberries with the water and sugar until tender, about 10 min. Purée in a food processor or blender then stir in the vinegar and mint. Keep warm if required straight away.
3 ♦ Dip each portion of Camembert into the flour, then the beaten egg and then the breadcrumbs. Coat again in egg and bread-crumbs to ensure the cheese is well coated.
4 ♦ Reheat the sauce if necessary. Heat the oil and deep-fry the cheese for 1-1½ min until golden. Drain on kitchen paper (paper towels).
5 ♦ Garnish the Camembert with mint leaves and serve immediately with the hot sauce.

225g/8oz firm Camembert cheese
10ml/2tsp plain flour
  (all-purpose flour)
1 egg, beaten
25g/1oz dried breadcrumbs
oil for deep frying
sprigs mint to garnish

for the sauce:
450g/1lb gooseberries, topped
  and tailed
150ml/¹/4pt/²/3 cup water
30ml/2tbsp/3tbsp sugar, or to
  taste
30ml/2tbsp/3tbsp white wine
  vinegar
10ml/2tsp chopped mint

CRAB MOUSSE
Serves 4

Cooked fresh or canned salmon or tuna can be used instead of crab if preferred.

1 ♦ Cream the cheese by beating well until light and fluffy.
2 ♦ Chop the crab meat very finely in food processor and add the softened butter, seasoning, lemon juice and blend in the cream cheese. Process until smooth then gently fold in the whipped cream.
3 ♦ Divide the mixture between 4 individual dishes and smooth the tops. Chill before serving with lemon wedges and garnish with a little chopped parsley.

175g/6oz cream cheese
350g/12oz crab meat, fresh,
  canned or frozen, thawed
20g/³/4oz butter, softened
salt and pepper
few drops lemon juice
65ml/2¹/2fl oz/¹/3 cup double
  or whipping cream, whipped
lemon and chopped parsley for
  serving

Baked Sardines With Garlic and Wine
Serves 4

1 ◆ Preheat the oven to 210°C/gas 7.
2 ◆ Place the oil in a shallow ovenproof dish. Dry the sardines and place head to tail in the oil. Brush some of the oil over the fish, sprinkle with the garlic and add the lemon juice and wine to the dish.
3 ◆ Bake the sardines for 20-30 min until sizzling. Garnish with chopped parsley and serve straight away from the dish, with crusty bread.

30ml/2tbsp/3tbsp olive oil
450-550g/1-1¹/4lb fresh
  sardines, cleaned and washed
2-3 cloves garlic, finely chopped
juice ¹/2 lemon
1 wine glass dry white wine
15ml/1tbsp chopped parsley
crusty bread for serving

Tagliatelle With Garlic and Herb Sauce
Serves 2–3

Use ready-made garlic and herb cheese for the easy base sauce then combine with freshly cooked pasta for a simply delicious texture and creamy taste.

1 ◆ Cook the pasta in a large saucepan of boiling, salted water with the oil until al dente (it should be firm in texture but with no hard core).
2 ◆ Meanwhile, turn the garlic and herb cheese into a large saucepan. Heat gently, stirring in the cream or milk gradually to make a smooth sauce.
3 ◆ Add a little of the pasta water to the sauce if necessary, to make a fairly thin consistency. Season to taste.
4 ◆ Drain the pasta and run under tepid water to refresh. Drain well then toss in the sauce to coat lightly. Serve immediately, sprinkled with chopped parsley.

175g/6oz tagliatelle
15ml/1tbsp oil
100-150g/4-5oz soft garlic and
  herb cheese eg Boursin
45-60ml/3-4tbsp/4-5tbsp single
  cream (light cream) or top of the
  milk
salt and freshly ground black
  pepper
chopped parsley for garnish

(*From top*) Baked Sardines with Garlic and Wine; Tagliatelle with Garlic and Herb Sauce

TOMATOES STUFFED WITH CHEESE AND BASIL
Serves 3–6

6 medium tomatoes
100g/4oz mozzarella cheese,
  grated
fresh basil
175g/6oz rindless goat's cheese
  (or soft creamy cheese)
salt and freshly ground black
  pepper
salad leaves for garnish
french dressing (page 40),
  optional
sesame and lemon bread for
  serving, optional

1 • Cut a small, thin slice from the bottom of each tomato (opposite the stalk) and discard. Carefully scoop out the seeds and flesh using a teaspoon or sharp knife. Discard the pulp and reserve the strained juices. Turn the tomatoes upside down for a few minutes to drain.

2 • Mix together the mozzarella and basil and blend with the goat's cheese. Season to taste and use to fill the centres of the tomatoes.

3 • Place the stuffed tomatoes in a dish or on a baking tray and cook at 180°C/gas 4 for about 20 min until lightly cooked and the cheese melted. Brown them under a grill if preferred.

4 • Garnish with salad leaves and serve with french dressing and sesame and lemon bread if liked.

SESAME AND LEMON BREAD
Serves 4–6

1 french loaf
100g/4oz butter
30ml/2tbsp/3tbsp lemon juice
5ml/1tsp grated lemon rind
30-45ml/2-3tbsp/3-4tbsp
  sesame seeds

1 • Cut the french loaf, not quite through, into slices about 2.5cm/1in thick.

2 • Soften the butter then beat in the lemon juice and rind. Spread the slices with the lemon butter and sprinkle with sesame seeds.

3 • Wrap the loaf in foil, leaving a small gap in the foil on the top, and bake at 180-200°C/gas 4-6 for 10-15 min. Serve hot.

STIR-FRIED VEGETABLES WITH ALMONDS
Serves 2–3

Stir-fried vegetables make an excellent starter. The ingredients may be varied to what's available – just make sure they are cooked to a delicious crispness.

1 ♦ Heat the oil in a wok or large pan, add the almonds and cook, stirring until golden. Remove from the pan with a draining spoon and set aside.
2 ♦ Add the ginger and garlic to the pan and fry for about 1 min. Add the carrot, leek, pepper, mange-tout and fry for 3-4 min, stirring continuously with a wooden spatula to toss the vegetables over. Stir in the courgettes and bean sprouts.
3 ♦ Mix together the remaining ingredients, pour over the vegetables and stir well again. Cook vigorously for a couple of minutes to steam the vegetables.
4 ♦ Check the seasoning, stir in the almonds and serve straight away.

30ml/2tbsp/3tbsp oil
50g/2oz blanched almonds
10mm/¹/₂in piece root ginger, finely chopped
1-2 cloves garlic, finely chopped
1 carrot, cut into julienne strips
1 leek, sliced
1 red or yellow pepper, sliced
75g/3oz mange-tout
1-2 courgettes, sliced
75-100g/3-4oz bean sprouts
10ml/2tsp tomato purée
10ml/2tsp soy sauce
30ml/2tbsp/3tbsp medium sherry
30ml/2tbsp/3tbsp water
salt and pepper to taste

SWISS CHEESE FONDUE
Serves 4–6

1 ♦ Rub the garlic around the inside of a heatproof dish or saucepan over a low heat and warm the wine and lemon juice.
2 ♦ Add grated cheese to the dish, stirring until the cheese and wine blend together.
3 ♦ Add the cornflour (cornstarch), blended with the kirsch and the seasonings, and continue to cook for 2-3 min, until the fondue thickens.
4 ♦ Serve, keeping the fondue warm over a small spirit lamp or dish warmer, with cubes of crusty bread for dipping.

1 clove garlic, crushed
150ml/¹/₄pt/²/₃ cup dry white wine and a squeeze of lemon juice
225g/8oz Emmenthal cheese, grated
10ml/2tsp cornflour (cornstarch)
1 liqueur glass kirsch
a little pepper
nutmeg, grated

BEEF SATAYS WITH PEANUT SAUCE
Serves 4–6

*150ml/ 1/4pt/ 2/3 cup boiling
   water*
*45ml/ 3tbsp/ 4tbsp desiccated
   coconut*
*450g/ 1lb rump steak, trimmed of
   fat*
*1 small onion, very finely chopped
   or minced (ground)*
*1 clove garlic, crushed with a little
   salt*
pinch chilli powder
30ml/ 2tbsp/ 3tbsp soy sauce
45ml/ 3tbsp/ 4tbsp peanut butter

*Pork or chicken can replace the beef if preferred. The satays are
quickly prepared but allow at least 2 hours for the meat to marinate.*

1 ◆ Pour the boiling water over the desiccated coconut and leave to
   infuse for 15 min.
2 ◆ Cut the meat into small 1.25cm/1/2in cubes and place into
   shallow dish.
3 ◆ Strain the coconut liquid and mix with the remaining ingredients.
4 ◆ Pour the marinade over the meat, cover and leave in a cool place
   for at least 2 hr or refrigerate overnight, stirring occasionally.
5 ◆ Remove the meat from the marinade and thread on to small
   skewers.
6 ◆ Cook under a medium/hot grill, turning occasionally and basting
   with the marinade.
7 ◆ While the satays are cooking, gently simmer the remaining
   marinade, adding a little water to thin if necessary, and serve
   with the satays.

MIXED NOODLE SALAD
WITH SMOKED CHICKEN
Serves 4–6

*175-225g/ 6-8oz fresh green and
   white egg noodles*
10ml/ 2tsp oil
*45-60ml/ 3-4tbsp/ 4-5tbsp
   French dressing (see page 40), or
   to taste*
*225g/ 8oz smoked chicken, thinly
   sliced*
*fresh-grated Parmesan cheese to
   taste*
*few sprigs basil or thinly sliced red
   pepper to garnish*

1 ◆ Cook the noodles in plenty of boiling salted water with the oil for
   about 2-3 min or until al dente. Drain well and refresh with tepid
   water.
2 ◆ While the noodles are still warm, add about half of the dressing
   and toss really well (it's easier with your hands), so that the
   noodles absorb some of the dressing. Gradually add more
   dressing to taste.
3 ◆ Arrange the noodles in individual serving bowls and arrange the
   slices of smoked chicken over the top. Toss very lightly.
4 ◆ Sprinkle with grated Parmesan cheese, garnish with basil or
   thinly sliced red pepper and serve straight away.

(From top) Mixed Noodle Salad with Smoked Chicken; Beef Satays with
Peanut Sauce; Stir-fried Vegetables with Almonds

60ml/4tbsp/5tbsp olive oil
15ml/1tbsp white wine vinegar
5ml/1tsp lemon juice
5ml/1tsp grated lemon rind
2.5ml/¹/2tsp soft brown sugar
salt and freshly ground black
 pepper
2.5ml/1¹/2tsp Dijon mustard

FRENCH DRESSING

Place all the ingredients into a food processor or blender and process until smooth, or whisk vigorously in a bowl, or place into a screw-top jar and shake well.

POTTED PRAWNS WITH BASIL
Serves 4

225g/8oz unsalted butter
225g/8oz peeled prawns
freshly ground black pepper
15ml/1tsp fresh chopped basil or
 2.5ml/¹/2tsp dried basil
lemon wedges for garnish

1 ◆ Melt 150g/5oz butter in a saucepan over a gentle heat. Add the prawns and cook for a few minutes.
2 ◆ Purée the prawns with the butter until smooth. Add basil and pepper to taste.
3 ◆ Press the mixture into individual ramekin dishes and chill until firm.
4 ◆ Melt the remaining butter and pour over prawn mixture.
5 ◆ Chill until required. Garnish with lemon and serve with fingers of toast.

MARINATED KING PRAWNS
IN DILL DRESSING WITH MELON
Serves 4

150ml/¹/4pt/²/3 cup olive oil
15ml/1tbsp white wine vinegar
2 shallots, finely chopped
1 small clove garlic, finely chopped
pinch sugar
15ml/1tbsp Dijon mustard
salt and freshly ground black
 pepper
12 or 16 king prawns, peeled
30ml/2tbsp/3tbsp chopped dill
1 Ogen melon
sprigs dill for garnish

1 ◆ Whisk together the olive oil, vinegar, shallots, garlic, sugar, mustard, salt and pepper. Shake well in a screw-top jar or mix in a food processor. Leave in the refrigerator for 2 hr for flavours to blend.
2 ◆ Strain the marinade through a sieve and pour over the prawns. Add the dill and mix well. Cover and marinade in the refrigerator for a couple of hours or so.
3 ◆ Peel the melon, cut in halves and remove the seeds. Cut carefully into thin slices.
4 ◆ When ready to serve, remove the prawns from the marinade and brush the melon slices lightly with some of the marinade.
5 ◆ Arrange the melon slices and prawns on to serving plates and garnish each one with a sprig of dill.

SCALLOP AND MONKFISH KEBABS
Serves 4–6

Vary the mixture of fish to create different kebabs but use firm fish such as swordfish, tuna or halibut which will not fall apart on the skewers. Paprika (5ml/1tsp) or cumin (10ml/2tsp) can be added to the marinade to impart different flavours if liked.

8 scallops
450g/1lb monkfish
60ml/4tbsp/5tbsp olive oil
juice 1/2 lemon
1/2 onion, grated
salt and freshly ground black
  pepper
bay leaves, optional
chives, red pepper curls and lime
  for garnish

1 ♦ Cut the scallops into halves and the monkfish into 2.5-4cm/1-1½in cubes and place into a bowl or dish.
2 ♦ Mix together the olive oil, lemon, onion and seasoning and pour over the fish. Cover the dish and leave to marinate for at least an hour, turning the fish over occasionally.
3 ♦ Thread the scallops and monkfish alternately on to skewers with a flat or twisted blade, putting a bay leaf between each piece of fish if liked to give fragrance.
4 ♦ Cook under a medium hot grill for 8-10 min until just done, brushing them from time to time with the marinade and turning them as necessary.
5 ♦ Serve at once with the garnishes.

PROSCIUTTO AND STRAWBERRY PLATTER
Serves 4

100g/4oz prosciutto (or Parma
  ham), thinly sliced
75-100g/3-4oz large salami
  slices
75-100g/3-4oz small salami
  slices
100-150g/4-5oz strawberries,
  sliced

for the strawberry mustard:
50g/2oz strawberries
10ml/2tsp wholegrain mustard
5ml/1tsp olive oil
5ml/1tsp lemon juice
few fresh herbs for garnish

1 ♦ Roll the sliced prosciutto and arrange on one quarter of each of the small serving plates.
2 ♦ Arrange the salami slices around the edge of the plates and fill the centres with the sliced strawberries.
3 ♦ For the strawberry mustard, purée the strawberries in a food processor or blender or rub through a sieve. Mix with the mustard, olive oil and lemon juice and blend well together.
4 ♦ Serve the strawberry mustard separately or on the side with the prosciutto and garnish each platter with a few fresh herbs.

(Overleaf, from top) Prosciutto and Strawberry Platter; Scallop and Monkfish Kebabs; Marinated King Prawns in Dill Dressing with Melon

1/2 frisé or curly endive lettuce,
 washed and torn into bite-size
 pieces
a few radichio leaves, washed and
 torn into bite-size pieces
1/2 bunch watercress, washed and
 divided into sprigs
75-100g/3-4oz button
 mushrooms, wiped and finely
 sliced
50g/2oz walnuts, roughly
 chopped
60ml/4tbsp/5tbsp olive or walnut
 oil
1 shallot, chopped
350g/12oz chicken livers,
 trimmed and cut into pieces
4-5 lean bacon rashers, derinded
30ml/2tbsp/3tbsp red wine
 vinegar
30ml/2tbsp/3tbsp cranberry
 sauce
salt and freshly ground black
 pepper

WARM CHICKEN LIVER SALAD
WITH CRANBERRY DRESSING
Serves 4–6

*Warm salads are so reminiscent of French cuisine and they can be
varied according to the ingredients available.*

1 • Toss together the lettuce, radichio, watercress, mushrooms and
 walnuts and arrange in a salad bowl.
2 • Heat the oil in a frying-pan and lightly sauté the shallot for
 2-3 min or until just soft.
3 • Add the chicken livers and cook for about 5 min, stirring gently,
 until brown but still slightly pink inside.
4 • In the meantime, cook the bacon under a hot grill until crispy.
5 • Using a draining spoon, remove the livers from the pan and keep
 warm.
6 • Add the vinegar and cranberry sauce to the pan and stir well to
 blend. Bring to the boil and add the seasoning.
7 • Stir well and allow to boil for about 1 min until the liquid is
 slightly reduced and syrupy.
8 • Top the salad with the chicken livers, sprinkle with the dressing
 and toss lightly. Crumble or snip the bacon over the top and
 serve straightaway.

MUSHROOMS A LA GRECQUE
Serves 4

60ml/4tbsp/5tbsp olive oil
1 large onion, chopped
1 clove garlic, crushed
45ml/3tbsp/4tbsp tomato purée
45ml/3tbsp/4tbsp wine vinegar
275ml/1/2pt/11/4 cup water
1 wine glass red wine
seasoning
675g/11/2lb button mushrooms
chopped parsley for garnish

1 • Lightly fry the onion and garlic in oil.
2 • Add all other ingredients except mushrooms and parsley. Bring
 to the boil, cover and simmer for 15 min.
3 • Add the mushrooms to the sauce, cover and simmer for 5-10 min
 until tender.
4 • Serve hot or cold garnished with chopped parsley.

(*Previous page, from top*) Warm Chicken Liver Salad with Cranberry
Dressing; Scrambled Eggs with Prawns on Rye

SCRAMBLED EGGS WITH PRAWNS ON RYE
Serves 2–4

This is a variation of the more usual breakfast dish of scrambled eggs with smoked salmon – served with buck's fizz of course! It's really good served as a starter too.

1 • Beat the eggs lightly and stir in the cream (or yoghurt).
2 • Melt the butter over a gentle heat, add the egg mixture and black pepper to taste. Cook slowly stirring all the time and add the prawns (or smoked salmon).
3 • When the eggs begin to thicken, remove the pan from the heat and continue to stir until thickened sufficiently to taste.
4 • Spoon on to buttered slices rye bread and serve immediately, garnished if liked with thin lemon or lime slices, extra prawns and parsley sprigs.

5-6 eggs
45ml/3tbsp/4tbsp double cream (heavy cream) (or Greek thick natural yoghurt)
25g/1oz butter
black pepper
75g/3oz peeled prawns (or shredded smoked salmon)
slices of buttered rye bread
thin slices of lemon or lime, extra prawns and sprigs parsley for garnish, optional

SMOKED HADDOCK CROUSTADES
Serves 4

1 • Place the haddock, milk and bay leaf in a shallow pan over moderate heat. Cover and simmer gently for 10-12 min or until the fish flakes easily.
2 • Remove the bay leaf, strain the milk and reserve. Flake the fish.
3 • Melt the butter in a pan. Stir in the flour, pepper and mustard. Cook for 2 min then gradually stir in the reserved milk.
4 • Cook the sauce, stirring until thickened.
5 • Add the fish, about two-thirds each of the prawns and the parsley to the sauce and cook for 1 min.
6 • Toast the bread on both sides until golden. Divide the fish mixture between the toasts and garnish with the remaining prawns and parsley. Serve straight away.

225g/8oz smoked haddock, skinned and boned
275ml/1/2pt/11/4 cups milk
1 bay leaf
25g/1oz butter
25g/1oz flour
black pepper
5ml/1tsp wholegrain mustard
75g/3oz peeled prawns
30ml/2tbsp/3tbsp chopped parsley
about 1/2 small French stick, cut into thin slices

Chicken Tikka Salad With Raita Sauce
Serves 3–4

350-450g/12-16oz ready
 prepared chicken tikka pieces
1 x 425g/15oz can chickpeas (or
 black-eyed beans), drained
4-6 tomatoes, finely sliced
1/2 iceberg lettuce, finely shredded
50g/2oz almonds or cashew nuts,
 toasted
10ml/2tsp cumin seeds, toasted
6-8 spring onions
coriander leaves for garnish

for the sauce:
150ml/1/4pt/2/3 cup natural
 yoghurt
30-45ml/2-3tbsp/3-4tbsp
 coarsely grated cucumber
15ml/1tbsp chopped mint
pinch each ground cumin and
 cayenne
salt and freshly ground black
 pepper
fried or grilled poppadums for
 serving, optional

*The sauce may be combined with the chicken tikka and chickpeas –
as a dressing – before arranging on the lettuce if preferred.*

1 • Cut the chicken pieces into slices or leave whole as preferred and combine with the chickpeas.
2 • Arrange the tomatoes around the edge of a large serving bowl or individual dishes with the lettuce in the centre.
3 • Arrange the chicken and chickpeas on top of the lettuce and sprinkle with the toasted nuts and cumin. Cover the salad and set to one side to allow flavours to blend.
4 • Meanwhile, cut through the ends of the spring onions and soak in cold water to curl.
5 • For the sauce, beat or whisk the yoghurt until smooth and creamy then combine with the rest of the ingredients. Cover and refrigerate until required.
6 • Drain the spring onions and dry. Use them to decorate the salads with the coriander leaves. Place spoonsful of the sauce on the salads or hand round separately. Serve with crispy poppadums if liked.

Prawns in Garlic
Serves 4

4-5 cloves garlic (or to taste),
 finely chopped
1/2-1 small dried or fresh chilli
 pepper, deseeded and chopped
 or a pinch of cayenne
60ml/4tbsp/5tbsp olive oil
225-350g/8-12oz peeled prawns
salt
30ml/2tbsp/3tbsp chopped
 parsley
lemon wedges for serving

1 • Fry the garlic and pepper in the oil. As soon as the garlic begins to turn brown, add the prawns and salt to taste.
2 • Cook over a high heat, shaking the pan now and again, for about 2 min until sizzling hot.
3 • Serve straight from the pan sprinkled with parsley and accompanied by lemon wedges.

Note: If preferred, after stage 1, the prawns and the garlicky oil can be placed into individual ovenproof gratin dishes and heated in a hot oven until sizzling. Garnish each dish with parsley and serve with lemon wedges.

(From top) Chicken Tikka Salad with Raita Sauce; Pasta, Smoked Salmon and Dill Salad; Prawns in Garlic

PASTA, SMOKED SALMON AND DILL SALAD
Serves 2

75g/3oz pasta spirals or spaghetti
10ml/2tsp oil
75g/3oz smoked salmon, sliced
10-15ml/2-3tsp choped dill
marjoram leaves for garnish

for the dressing:
30ml/2tbsp/3tbsp oil
10ml/2tsp lemon juice
salt and freshly ground black
 pepper

Spaghetti can be used as an alternative to pasta spirals. Try different flavoured pastas for their colourful effect.

1 • If used, break the spaghetti strands into halves for easier handling. Cook the pasta in plenty of boiling, salted water with the oil until al dente – about 8-10 min if dried or 3-4 min if fresh.
2 • Drain the pasta well, rinse with tepid water and drain again. Leave to cool, shaking and turning it over occasionally.
3 • For the dressing, whisk together the oil and lemon juice with salt and freshly ground black pepper to taste.
4 • Cut the smoked salmon into thin strips and combine with the spaghetti, chopped dill and sufficient of the dressing to taste.
5 • Toss the salad over lightly and serve on individual plates, garnishing each plate with marjoram leaves.

225g/8oz monkfish fillet, sliced
juice of 2 limes and a little grated
 rind
40 mussels in their shells, scraped
 and thoroughly washed
225g/8oz peeled prawns
12 quails' eggs, hard-boiled,
 shelled and halved
(or 6 hens' eggs, hard-boiled,
 shelled and quartered)
8 prawns in their shells

for the dressing:
45ml/3tbsp/4tbsp olive oil
30ml/2tbsp/3tbsp chopped
 parsley
freshly ground black pepper
chives and curls of lime rind for
 garnish

MARINATED SEAFOOD SALAD
Serves 6

A mélange of seafood in a simple dressing with tangy lime juice makes a sophisticated appetiser.

1 • Place the monkfish in a shallow dish with the lime juice and sprinkle with a little grated lime rind.
2 • Cover and leave in the refrigerator for 3-4 hr, turning occasionally.
3 • Cook the mussels in boiling salted water for 5-6 min. Drain and rinse, discarding any which do not open.
4 • Remove half the mussels from their shells and mix with the monkfish, peeled prawns and quails' eggs. Add the mussels and prawns in their shells.
5 • Arrange the salad on to serving plates, mix the ingredients for the dressing and pour over the top. Garnish with chives and curls of lime rind.

FIELD MUSHROOMS WITH CRAB STUFFING
Serves 4

The big flat field mushrooms have the best flavour and they also have larger bases to hold the filling.

1 ⬧ Melt the butter in a large non-stick fry-pan and sauté the mushrooms in a single layer – in two batches if necessary – until only just tender. Drain well on kitchen paper (paper towels) then sprinkle with salt and pepper.
2 ⬧ Divide the crab meat between the mushrooms, spread over the top of each one and sprinkle with the cheese and paprika.
3 ⬧ Brown under a hot grill and place each mushroom on a round of toast. Sprinkle with parsley and serve hot.

40g/1¹/₂oz butter
4 or 8 large flat mushrooms, 350-450g/12-16oz
salt and freshly ground black pepper
225g/8oz crab meat
50-75g/2-3oz Cheddar cheese, grated
paprika for sprinkling
4 rounds of toasted bread, buttered
15ml/1tbsp chopped parsley for garnish

GOUJONS OF COD
Serves 4–6

1 ⬧ Slice each fillet of cod in half lengthways. Make slanting cuts along the length of each half fillet, cutting the fish into narrow strips.
2 ⬧ Coat each strip in seasoned flour. Mix together the lightly beaten egg and vegetable oil.
3 ⬧ Dip the fish pieces in the egg mixture, then roll in breadcrumbs.
4 ⬧ Fry in the hot oil until crisp and golden brown. Drain on kitchen paper (paper towel).
5 ⬧ Garnish with wedges of fresh lemon. Serve with a green salad and crusty bread.

450-675g/1-1¹/₂lb cod, skinned and filleted
seasoned flour
1 egg, lightly beaten
15ml/1tbsp vegetable oil
dried breadcrumbs
oil for deep frying
seasoning
lemon wedges for garnish

MAIN COURSES

ROAST FILLET OF LAMB WITH ROSEMARY AND GARLIC
Serves 3–4

450g/1lb neck fillet of lamb
2-3 cloves garlic, finely chopped
15-25ml/1-1¹/₂tbsp/1-2tbsp
 finely chopped rosemary
salt and freshly ground black
 pepper
8 rashers streaky bacon, derinded
oil for brushing
10ml/2tsp flour
275ml/¹/₂pt/1¹/₄ cups chicken or
 vegetable stock
10ml/2tsp mild mustard
gravy browning, optional
lime wedges and herbs for garnish
new potatoes and mixed salad
 leaves for serving, optional

1 ◦ Cut the fillet into 3-4 pieces, then slice each piece lengthways but not all the way through. Open out the pieces and sprinkle with the garlic, rosemary and seasoning. Close up the fillets.
2 ◦ Stretch out the bacon rashers with a blunt knife and wrap around the fillets, securing with wooden cocktail sticks. Brush with oil, place in a small tin and roast at 200° C/gas 6 for 30-40 min or until tender.
3 ◦ Measure 30ml/2tbsp/3tbsp of the juices from the tin into a saucepan and stir in the flour. Cook over a medium to high heat until lightly browned then stir in the stock and mustard. Add a dash of gravy browning if liked.
4 ◦ Cook the gravy until thickened and boiling then simmer for about 5 min. Add seasoning to taste.
5 ◦ Slice the lamb into 6-12mm/¹/₄-¹/₂in pieces and serve with lime and herbs for garnish. New potatoes and mixed salad leaves go well with the lamb.

PORK IN A CRISPY COAT WITH APPLE RINGS
Serves 2

2 egg yolks
10ml/2tsp milk
40g/1¹/₂oz fresh breadcrumbs
15ml/1tbsp finely chopped mint
2 boneless pork chops or cutlets,
 about 150-175g/5-6oz each
30ml/2tbsp/3tbsp oil
2 small dessert apples
salt and freshly ground black
 pepper
sprigs of mint to garnish

1 ◦ Beat together the egg yolks and milk. Mix the breadcrumbs and chopped mint together and spread out on a plate.
2 ◦ Season the chops and dip firstly into the milk and egg yolk mixture, then coat with the minted breadcrumbs pressing them well into the surface of the chops.
3 ◦ Heat the oil in a fry-pan, add the chops and sauté for 10-15 min, turning once, until golden and tender. Transfer to a hot serving plate and keep warm.
4 ◦ In the meantime, core and slice the apple into rings. Quickly fry the apple slices until golden. Drain on kitchen paper (paper towels) and arrange beside the chops.
5 ◦ Garnish the plate with the sprigs of mint and serve straight away.

VEAL WITH CAPERS AND SOURED CREAM
Serves 4

1 ◆ Add seasoning to half the flour and use to coat the veal escalopes.
2 ◆ Heat 25g/1oz of the butter with the olive oil in a frying-pan and gently fry the veal for about 5 min on each side until golden and tender. Remove from the pan and set to one side.
3 ◆ Melt the remaining butter and sauté the onion until soft. Stir in the rest of the flour and cook for about 1 min.
4 ◆ Add the capers with their vinegar and water, stir well and cook until thickened. Stir in the soured cream and adjust seasoning.
5 ◆ Return the veal to the pan and heat through gently. Sprinkle with parsley and serve straight from the pan with freshly cooked egg noodles or tagliatelle.

salt and freshly ground black pepper
30ml/2tbsp/3tbsp plain flour (all-purpose flour)
4 veal escalopes
50g/2oz butter
15ml/1tbsp olive oil
1 small onion, finely chopped
30ml/2tbsp/3tbsp capers with their vinegar
150ml/1/4pt/2/3 cup water
150ml/1/4pt/2/3 cup soured cream
chopped parsley to garnish
egg noodles or tagliatelle for serving

RED MULLET IN VINE LEAVES
Serves 4

The mullet are cooked under the grill but they are also particularly good cooked on the barbeque. Ask the fishmonger to clean and bone the fish for you.

1 ◆ Blanch the vine leaves in boiling water for 3 min. Drain and refresh under cold water then pat dry with kitchen paper (paper towels).
2 ◆ Lay open the fish and remove any remaining large bones. Sprinkle with salt and pepper, the chopped dill and lemon juice.
3 ◆ Close up the fish and wrap in the vine leaves, securing with wooden cocktail sticks as necessary.
4 ◆ Brush liberally with olive oil and cook under a medium hot grill for 4-5 min each side.
5 ◆ Serve with lemon wedges, sprigs dill and salad if liked.

4 large vine leaves, fresh or preserved
4 large red mullet, cleaned, scaled and boned
salt and freshly ground black pepper
20ml/4tsp chopped fresh dill
20ml/4tsp lemon juice
olive oil for brushing
lemon wedges and sprigs dill for garnish
salad of tomatoes, onions, olives, feta cheese and oregano for serving, optional

Previous page (*Clockwise from left*) Roast Fillet of Lamb with Rosemary and Garlic; Pork in a Crispy Coat with Apple Rings; Veal with Capers and Soured Cream; Red Mullet in Vine Leaves

RACK OF LAMB WITH CUMBERLAND SAUCE
Serves 2

1 ◆ Thinly pare the rind from a quarter of the orange and cut it into thin shreds. Place the rind with the water in a pan and cook gently until tender. Drain and rinse well.
2 ◆ Squeeze and strain the juice from the orange. Heat the redcurrant jelly in a pan then whisk in the strained orange juice, lemon juice and port. Leave until cold and stir in the orange rind.
3 ◆ Cut away the main bone and trim the meat from cutlet bones back about 1.5cm/½in to expose the ends of the bones. Weigh the joint and place in a roasting tin.
4 ◆ Roast in a preheated oven at 180°C/gas 4 allowing 18-20 min per ½kg/1lb for a medium result. Increase the temperature to 200°C/gas 6 for the last 15 min to increase browning if preferred.
5 ◆ Cut the lamb into portions and place a cutlet frill on each bone tip. Garnish and serve straight away with the cold Cumberland sauce.

for the sauce:
1 orange
150ml/¼pt/⅔ cup boiling water
60ml/4tbsp/5tbsp redcurrant jelly
½ lemon, juice
1 liqueur glass port

for the rack of lamb:
1 best end of neck, chined and barked
oil for brushing
orange shreds and slices for garnish
cutlet frills for decoration

DUCK WITH PORT AND CRANBERRY SAUCE
Serves 2

1 ◆ Season the flour with salt and pepper and use to coat the duck.
2 ◆ Heat the oil in a saucepan, add the duck and fry for 10-12 min, turning once, until golden. Remove from the pan and drain off the oil and fat from the juices.
3 ◆ Mix the ginger, spring onion, cranberries and port together in the pan. Add the duck, cover and simmer for about 30 min, until tender.
4 ◆ Transfer the duck to a warm serving plate and keep warm.
5 ◆ Add the sauce to a blender or food processor and process until smooth. Adjust the seasoning to taste, adding sugar if required, and reheat in the pan if necessary.
6 ◆ Spoon the sauce over the duck. Garnish with chives and serve with a watercress or green salad.

30ml/2tbsp/3tbsp plain flour (all-purpose flour)
salt and freshly ground black pepper
2 duck breast with wing portions
30ml/2tbsp/3tbsp oil
12mm/½in piece fresh root ginger, chopped finely
30ml/2tbsp/3tbsp finely sliced spring onion
175g/6oz cranberries
150-175ml/5-7fl oz/⅔-1 cup port
10-15ml/2-3tsp sugar, optional
finely sliced chives for garnish
watercress or green salad for serving

(*From top*) Rack of Lamb with Cumberland Sauce; Duck with Port and Cranberry Sauce

BAKED PORK WITH ORANGE AND CARDAMOM
Serves 4

15-30ml/1-2tbsp/1-3tbsp oil
4 pork chops, about
  175-200g/6-7oz each
1 medium onion, thinly sliced
4 large oranges
3ml/³/4tsp ground cardamom
salt and freshly ground black
  pepper
curls of orange rind and chopped
  parsley for garnish

The chops are lightly fried before baking – take care not to overcook
at this stage or the flesh will toughen.

1 ♦ Heat the oil in a large heatproof casserole and fry the chops briskly on both sides to brown lightly. Add the onion and sauté for a further 3-4 min.
2 ♦ Grate the rind of one orange and squeeze the juice from all the oranges – about 275ml/½pt/1¼ cups. Add to the dish with the cardamom and salt and pepper to taste.
3 ♦ Bring to the boil then cover and cook in a preheated oven at 190°C/gas 5 for about 30 min or until the pork is tender.
4 ♦ Adjust the seasoning and serve with curls of orange rind and chopped parsley.

GAMMON WITH SPICY RAISIN SAUCE
Serves 2

30ml/2tbsp/3tbsp raisins
2 cloves
5cm/2in piece cinnamon stick
100ml/4fl oz/¹/2 cup natural
  pineapple juice
15ml/1tbsp light brown soft sugar
5ml/1tsp cornflour (cornstarch)
15ml/1tbsp water
10ml/2tsp lemon juice
salt and freshly ground black
  pepper
2 gammon steaks
15g/¹/2oz butter, melted
orange slices to garnish

1 ♦ Place the raisins, cloves, cinnamon stick and pineapple juice in a small saucepan, cover and simmer for 10 min. Discard the cloves and cinnamon.
2 ♦ Blend the sugar and cornflour (cornstarch) to a paste with the water, then gradually stir into the sauce and bring to the boil, stirring constantly. Stir in the lemon juice, and salt and pepper. Keep warm.
3 ♦ Snip the fat around the edges of the gammon steaks. Brush them with melted butter and cook the steaks under a preheated moderate grill for 6-7 min, turning once.
4 ♦ Serve straight away, with the sauce spooned over the gammon steaks and garnished with orange slices.

CHICKEN WITH ROSEMARY
Serves 4

1 • Heat the butter and olive oil in a large fry-pan with the garlic and rosemary.
2 • When the mixture begins to sizzle, add the chicken and sauté over a medium heat, turning the pieces until they are browned all over.
3 • Add seasoning and the wine then cover the pan and simmer for about 30 min or until the chicken is very tender.
4 • Remove the rosemary sprigs from the pan and replace with a few fresh sprigs for garnish. Serve hot, straight from the pan.

25-40g/1-1¹/₂oz butter
15ml/1tbsp olive oil
2-3 cloves garlic, sliced
3 medium sprigs rosemary
1 chicken, about 1¹/₂kg/3lb cut into quarters or 4 chicken portions
salt and freshly ground black pepper
175ml/6fl oz/³/4 cup dry white wine
sprigs rosemary for garnish

CALVES' LIVER WITH MUSTARD AND LIME SAUCE
Serves 4

1 • Trim the liver and remove any tubes or membrane. Dip the liver slices in seasoned flour.
2 • Heat the butter and oil until hot and briskly fry the liver for about 1-1½ min each side until brown on the outside and still slightly pink in the middle. Remove the liver from the pan and keep warm.
3 • Add the mustard, lime juice and rind to the pan and bring to the boil, stirring. Stir in half of the stock and the Worcestershire sauce.
4 • Bring to the boil, simmer vigorously to reduce slightly then add the remaining stock and reduce slightly again.
5 • Pour the sauce over the liver or replace the liver into the pan. Serve straight from the pan, garnished with slices of lime, curls of rind and parsley or chervil.

450g/1lb calves' liver (or lambs' liver), thinly sliced
seasoned flour
25g/1oz butter
15ml/1tbsp vegetable oil
15ml/1tbsp wholegrain mustard
1 lime, juice and freshly grated rind
150ml/¹/4pt/²/3 cup veal or beef stock, or water
10ml/2tsp Worcestershire sauce
slices lime and fine strips rind, to garnish
sprigs parsley or chervil to garnish

DEEP-FRIED CHICKEN WITH LEMON AND RUM
Serves 4

100ml/4fl oz/ 1/2 cup fresh
  lemon juice
50ml/2fl oz/ 1/4 cup light soy
  sauce
30ml/2tbsp/3tbsp dark rum
4 cloves garlic, finely chopped
1 chicken, about 2kg/ 4 1/2lb or
  chicken pieces
salt and freshly ground black
  pepper
plain flour (all-purpose flour)
  for dusting
425ml/ 3/4pt/2 cups vegetable
  oil for frying
1 lemon for serving
mixed leaves salad for serving

The chicken is marinated in lemon and rum before cooking.

1 • Mix together the first 4 ingredients for the marinade and place in a dish or bowl.
2 • Cut the chicken into about 8 portions, removing skin if preferred. Steep the pieces of chicken in the marinade, mixing well to coat. Cover and chill in the fridge for 4 hours or overnight, turning occasionally.
3 • Drain the chicken and pat dry with kitchen paper (paper towels). Season the pieces and dust with flour.
4 • Heat the oil in a deep-fat fryer or deep pan until hot. Carefully place half the chicken pieces in the oil and fry for about 10 min until golden brown. Drain on kitchen paper (paper towels) and keep warm.
5 • When the oil is hot again fry the remaining chicken pieces.
6 • Sprinkle with a little more lemon juice and seasoning and serve with a mixed salad and lemon slices.

PORK WITH MARSALA
Serves 4–6

1kg/2lb pork fillet
45ml/3tbsp/4tbsp oil
25g/1oz butter
salt and freshly ground black
  pepper
150-175ml/5-6fl. oz/ 2/3-3/4
  cup Marsala
a few green grapes and a small
  bunch herbs for garnish

This dish is so easy and uses Marsala but any dessert wine could be substituted.

1 • Cut the pork fillet into medallion slices. Fry a few slices at a time over a high heat in the oil and butter until lightly browned on each side.
2 • Replace the slices in the pan, sprinkle with seasoning and pour in the Marsala.
3 • Simmer for about 10 min until the pork is cooked and the liquid is reduced. Transfer to a hot serving dish and garnish with a few grapes and herbs.

(From top) Pork in Marsala; Deep-fried Chicken with Lemon and Rum; Calves' Liver with Mustard and Lime Sauce

GREEN TORTELLINI WITH MUSHROOMS AND CREAM
Serves 4

*450g/1lb ready prepared fresh
  green tortellini*
salt
*30ml/2tbsp/3tbsp olive oil,
  approximately*
40g/1¹/2oz butter
*350g/12oz button mushrooms,
  sliced*
*275ml/¹/2pt/1¹/4 cups crème
  fraîche or soured cream*
freshly ground black pepper
*fresh grated Parmesan cheese
  and salad leaves for serving*

1 • Cook the tortellini in a large pan of boiling water with salt and 15ml/1tbsp of the oil for about 5 min until al dente, then leave to stand for a few minutes.
2 • Meanwhile, melt the butter in a fry-pan and sauté the mushrooms until just tender but still a little firm. Remove the mushrooms from the pan with a slotted spoon and keep warm.
3 • Add the cream to the pan and gently heat, adding seasoning to taste. Bring to the boil, stirring and then simmer for a few minutes until reduced and thickened and slightly syrupy. Stir in the mushrooms.
4 • Drain the pasta and add a little extra oil, tossing over well. Pour the sauce over the tortellini and serve straight away with a bowl of grated Parmesan cheese and a side salad.

ITALIAN MEATBALLS
Serves 4

*500g/18oz lean minced beef
  (ground beef)*
15ml/1tbsp chopped oregano
1 small onion, very finely chopped
1-2 cloves of garlic, crushed
1 small lemon, finely grated rind
15g/¹/2oz fine fresh breadcrumbs
*salt and freshly ground black
  pepper*
pinch grated nutmeg
1 egg, lightly beaten
olive oil for frying
*buttered egg noodles or spaghetti,
  and fresh tomato sauce (page 27)
  for serving*
*freshly grated Parmesan cheese
  for serving*

1 • Mix the first 8 ingredients together well and bind the mixture together with the egg.
2 • If you have time, cover and chill for 1-6 hours to allow the flavours to blend.
3 • Divide the mixture with your hands and shape in balls about the size of golf balls.
4 • Shallow fry the meatballs in olive oil, turning frequently until browned and cooked through.
5 • Serve on a bed of buttered egg noodles or spaghetti as suggested above, with a tangy tomato sauce and plenty of grated Parmesan cheese sprinkled over the top.

TOGENBURGERS
Serves 2

1 • Mix the minced (ground) steak with the walnuts, onions and seasoning. Divide the mixture into two, shape into balls then press flat into rounds.
2 • Brush the top of each burger with oil or melted butter and cook under a medium hot grill for 8-10 min each side.
3 • Meanwhile, mix together the cheese, mustard and cream or yoghurt. Add seasoning and paprika to taste. Divide into 2 and form into flat patties with your hands.
4 • Season the spinach and heat gently in a pan. Drain well and add a knob of butter and a spoonful of cream or yoghurt if liked.
5 • Brush both sides of the rye bread with oil or melted butter. When the meat is cooked, toast both sides of the rye bread under a hot grill.
6 • Place the rye toast in the bottom of 2 individual gratin dishes. Top with the spinach, then the burgers, then the cheese patties.
7 • Cook under the grill until the cheese is melted and lightly browned. Serve straight away garnished with tomato slices if liked.

450g/1lb lean steak, minced (ground)
25g/1oz walnuts, finely chopped
1 small onion, finely chopped or minced (ground)
salt and freshly ground black pepper
oil or melted butter, for brushing
2 large thick slices of rye bread
100g/4oz Gruyère or Emmenthal cheese, finely grated
2.5-5ml/^{1}/2-1tsp mild mustard, to taste
30-45ml/2-3tbsp/3-4tbsp thick cream or natural yoghurt
paprika
225ml/8oz frozen leaf spinach, thawed
knob of butter and 1 heaped tsp thick cream or natural yoghurt, optional
sliced tomato for garnish, optional

GINGERED LAMB WITH LIME
Serves 2

1 • Heat the butter and oil in a fry-pan and gently cook the ginger and lime zest and juice for 6-8 min until slightly syrupy.
2 • Lightly season the steaks or chops and add to the hot pan, turning them over in the glaze.
3 • Cook gently for about 8 min each side, spooning the glaze over once or twice and turning the lamb over as necessary, until the lamb is lightly browned.
4 • Serve straight from the pan garnished with lime slices.

15g/^{1}/2oz butter
5ml/1tsp oil
2.5cm/1in piece root ginger, grated
5ml/1tsp grated lime zest (or lemon)
10ml/2tsp lime juice (or lemon)
2 lamb leg steaks or double loin chops
salt and freshly ground black pepper
lime (or lemon) slices for garnish

BEEF FILLET CHASSEUR
Serves 2

15ml/1tbsp olive oil
10ml/2tsp flour
salt and freshly ground black
  pepper
2 slices of lean beef fillet,
  about 175-200g/6-7oz each
1 small onion, finely chopped
1 clove garlic, finely chopped
10ml/2tsp fresh chopped
  herbs, parsley and thyme
150ml/¹/4pt/²/3 cup red wine
6 tomatoes, skinned and
  chopped or 90ml/6tbsp/8tbsp
  canned chopped tomatoes
10ml/2tsp tomato purée
1 bay leaf
75g/3oz mushrooms, finely
  sliced
chopped parsley for garnish

1 ◦ Heat the oil in a sauté- or fry-pan. Season the flour with salt and pepper and use to sprinkle over the fillets.
2 ◦ Arrange the fillets in the hot oil and cook for 1½ min each side. Remove the meat and keep warm.
3 ◦ Stir the onion and garlic into the pan and sauté until transparent. Add the herbs, wine, tomatoes and tomato purée and cook for 10-15 min until the tomatoes are just tender.
4 ◦ Return the fillets to the pan together with the bay leaf and mushrooms. Cover the pan and continue to cook gently for 20 min.
5 ◦ Remove the fillets with a draining spoon to a hot serving dish and keep warm. Heat the sauce briskly for 5 min or until thick and concentrated. Remove the bay leaf and adjust seasoning.
6 ◦ Serve with the sauce poured over the fillets, garnished with chopped parsley.

STEAK AU POIVRE VERT
Serves 4

Green peppercorns have a more subtle flavour than black ones.

4 fillet or entrecôte steaks
30ml/2tbsp/3tbsp green
  peppercorns, crushed
50g/2oz butter
30ml/2tbsp/3tbsp brandy,
  warmed
225ml/8fl oz/1 cup soured or
  single cream (sour or light
  cream)
salt to taste
sprigs watercress for garnish
mixed leaf salad with rich
  dressing (page 40) for
  serving

1 ◦ Trim the steaks as necessary and press the crushed peppercorns into both sides. Leave to stand for 15 min.
2 ◦ Heat the butter in the frying-pan and briskly fry the steaks for 2 min on each side. Lower the heat and cook for a further 3-6 min on each side, or cooked to taste. Transfer to a hot serving dish and keep warm.
3 ◦ Add the brandy to the juices in the pan and ignite. When the flames have died down, stir in the cream. Cook briskly for 2 min, stirring all the time. Add salt to taste.
4 ◦ Spoon the sauce over the steaks. Garnish with watercress and serve immediately with a mixed leaf salad tossed in a rich vinaigrette dressing.

(From top) Togenburger; Beef Fillet Chasseur; Steak au Poivre Vert

SAUTÉED CHICKEN IN CITRUS SAUCE
Serves 2

225g/8oz chicken breast fillet
seasoned flour
1 small orange
1 small grapefruit
60ml/4tbsp/5tbsp dry white wine
15ml/1tbsp chopped coriander
15ml/1tbsp oil
25g/1oz butter
pinch paprika
90ml/6tbsp/8tbsp double cream
  (heavy cream)
salt and freshly ground black
  pepper
orange and grapefruit slices and
  fresh coriander to garnish

1 • Cut the chicken into 5mm/¼in slices. Bat out into thin slices between two sheets of greaseproof paper (wax paper) or clingfilm (saran wrap), using a rolling pin. Dip the slices into the seasoned flour.
2 • Put 30ml/2tbsp/3tbsp orange and 30ml/2tbsp/3tbsp grapefruit juice into a small saucepan. Add the dry white wine and fresh coriander and boil until reduced by half.
3 • Meanwhile, heat the oil and butter in a medium sauté-pan and fry the chicken slices briskly for 2 min on each side or until cooked through.
4 • Add juice mixture, paprika and cream. Simmer gently for 1-2 min or until hot through. Adjust seasoning to taste and serve straight away garnished with the citrus fruits and coriander.

MEXICAN CHILLI BEANS
Serves 2–3

30ml/2tbsp/3tbsp oil
1 medium onion, finely chopped
2.5-5ml/½-1tsp chilli powder
  to taste
400g/14oz can chopped tomatoes
275ml/½pt/1¼ cups vegetable
  stock
5ml/1tsp mild mustard
15ml/1tbsp black treacle (dark
  molasses)
425g/15oz can red kidney beans,
  drained
425g/15oz can black-eyed
  beans, drained
salt and freshly ground black
  pepper
15ml/1tbsp chopped coriander or
  parsley
½ red or yellow pepper and 1
  avocado for garnish, optional

1 • Heat the oil and gently sauté the onion with the chilli powder until the onion is tender and starts to brown.
2 • Stir in the tomatoes, stock, mustard, treacle (molasses) and beans. Add seasoning to taste and simmer gently for 15-20 min uncovered.
3 • Stir in the coriander or parsley and simmer for a further 5 min. Adjust the seasoning.
4 • Dice the red or yellow pepper and when ready to serve, peel and slice the avocado. Garnish the dish with the pepper and avocado and serve with rice or garlic bread.

Pork Piquant
Serves 2

1 ◆ Cut the pork fillet into strips 1.25cm/¹/₂in wide.
2 ◆ Melt the butter in a small saucepan, add the ginger and fry gently for about 1 min.
3 ◆ Season the cornflour (cornstarch) and use to coat the pork strips. Add to the pan and fry for 1-2 min, stirring.
4 ◆ Stir in the remaining ingredients, bring to the boil, then cover and simmer for about 6 min until the pork is cooked.
5 ◆ Serve garnished with the shredded green spring onion.

225-275g/8-10oz pork fillet
40g/1¹/₂oz butter
10mm/¹/₂in piece fresh root ginger, finely chopped
15ml/1tbsp cornflour (cornstarch)
60ml/4tbsp/5tbsp frozen concentrated orange juice
30ml/2tbsp/3tbsp redcurrant jelly
60ml/4tbsp/5tbsp water
60ml/4tbsp/5tbsp finely sliced spring onions
salt and freshly ground black pepper
shredded spring onion (green part) for garnish

Lamb Chops Braised With Leeks and Lentils
Serves 4

The lamb is marinated before cooking.

1 ◆ Place the chops in a dish in a single layer. Sprinkle with the onions, wine and seasoning. Cover and refrigerate for 12 hr, turning the chops occasionally.
2 ◆ Remove the chops from the marinade and pat dry. Reserve the marinade.
3 ◆ Heat a little oil in a sauté-pan and quickly fry the chops until brown – a few minutes each side – then drain on kitchen paper (paper towels).
4 ◆ Place the leeks, lentils and paprika into the pan and stir over a medium heat for 2 min. Arrange the chops on top of the lentils.
5 ◆ Pour in the marinade and stock. Bring to the boil then cover and simmer for 20-30 min until tender. Serve garnished with coriander.

4 loin lamb chops, about 450g/1lb, trimmed
1 small onion, finely chopped
100ml/4fl oz/¹/₂ cup dry white wine
salt and freshly ground black pepper
oil for shallow frying
450g/1lb leeks (trimmed weight), sliced
100g/4oz red split lentils
5ml/1tsp paprika
275ml/¹/₂pt/1¹/₄ cups vegetable stock
fresh coriander to garnish
new potatoes for serving, optional

LAMBS' KIDNEYS IN BEER WITH CORIANDER
Serves 4

1 ♦ Heat the oil in a frying-pan and gently sauté the onion for 3-4 min until soft. Stir in the kidneys and continue to cook for about 8 min, stirring occasionally, until brown.
2 ♦ Add the flour, seasoning and ground coriander and stir well to blend. Stir in the orange rind and juice and beer.
3 ♦ Bring to the boil, stirring until thickened, then simmer for a further 3-4 min.
4 ♦ Serve sprinkled with crushed coriander and garnish with curls of orange rind and coriander leaves if liked.
5 ♦ Serve with boiled rice which has been moulded in lightly oiled ramekins, cups or dariole moulds.

30ml/2tbsp/3tbsp vegetable oil
1 large onion, chopped
450-675g/1-1¹/₂lb lambs'
 kidneys, cut in halves and cored
30ml/2tbsp/3tbsp plain flour
 (all-purpose flour)
salt and freshly ground black
 pepper
5ml/1tsp ground coriander
10ml/2tsp grated orange rind
30ml/2tbsp/3tbsp orange juice
275ml/¹/₂pt/1¹/₄ cups strong
 beer or ale
5ml/1tsp crushed coriander seeds
curls of orange rind and coriander
 leaves for garnish
fluffy boiled rice for serving

LAMB AND OLIVE PILAU
Serves 4

1 ♦ Heat the oil in a large sauté- or frying-pan and gently cook the onion until transparent. Stir in the rice or mixed grains and cook for a further minute, stirring.
2 ♦ Pour in the stock and add the lamb. Bring to the boil then cover and simmer for 20-30 min until the lamb is tender and the rice has absorbed most of the liquid. (The mixed grains with wild rice may need a little longer cooking time.) Stir from time to time and if necessary, add a little extra stock or water during the cooking.
3 ♦ About 5 min before the end of the cooking time, stir in the olives, chickpeas, cumin and seasoning to taste. Sprinkle with the pistachios, garnish with the olives if liked and serve straight away.

15ml/1tbsp oil
1 onion, finely chopped
175g/6oz brown rice or mixed
 rice grains with wild rice
425ml/³/₄pt/2 cups vegetable
 stock
450g/1lb lean lamb, diced
100g/4oz pitted black or green
 olives, cut into quarters
425g/15oz can chickpeas,
 drained
pinch of ground cumin
salt and freshly ground black
 pepper
50g/2oz pistachios
olives for garnish, optional
tomato and onion salad and
 pitta bread for serving,
 optional

(From top) Lambs' Kidneys in Beer with Coriander; Lamb and Olive Pilau; Lamb Chops Braised with Leeks and Lentils

SAUTÉ OF SALMON WITH ASPARAGUS
Serves 4

175g/6oz fine asparagus
450g/1lb salmon fillet, skinned
salt and freshly ground black
  pepper
50g/2oz butter
1 shallot, finely chopped
150ml/¹/4pt/²/3 cup dry white
  wine
150ml/¹/4pt/²/3 cup single cream
  (light cream)
15ml/1tbsp chervil, chopped
2 tomatoes, peeled, deseeded and
  chopped
sprigs chervil for garnish

1 ⋄ Slice the asparagus spears diagonally into 4cm/1½in lengths. Cook in gently simmering salted walter until just tender, drain.
2 ⋄ Cut salmon into portions, season to taste.
3 ⋄ Heat half of the butter in a sauté-pan. Add the shallot and cook until just transparent.
4 ⋄ Arrange the salmon in the pan and continue to cook gently for about 6 min, turning once, taking care not to overcook. Lift the salmon on to a hot serving dish with a fish-slice and keep warm.
5 ⋄ Stir the wine into the pan and boil briskly to reduce the quantity by half. Add the cream and simmer for 3-4 min.
6 ⋄ Whisk the remaining half of the butter into the sauce, add the asparagus, herbs and tomato and heat gently.
7 ⋄ Serve with the sauce spooned around the salmon and garnished with a little more chervil.

SCALLOPS PROVENCALE
Serves 3–4

675g/1¹/2lb scallops
flour for dredging
salt and freshly ground black
  pepper
45-60ml/3-4tbsp/4-5tbsp olive
  oil
2-3 cloves garlic, finely chopped
15-30ml/1-2tbsp/1-3tbsp
  brandy, optional
15ml/1tbsp finely chopped
  parsley

1 ⋄ Cut the scallops into halves leaving the corals intact. Season the flour with salt and pepper. Roll the scallops well in the flour.
2 ⋄ Heat the oil in a large sauté- or fry-pan and briskly fry the scallops with the garlic for about 2-3 min until just cooked and translucent. Take care not to overcook or the scallops will toughen.
3 ⋄ Add the brandy and parsley towards the end of cooking and serve straight away, direct from the pan.

SEAFOOD PAELLA
Serves 4

1 ◆ Place the saffron in a heatproof jug and pour over 75ml/ 2½fl oz/⅓ cup boiling water. Leave to soak for about 10 min, then strain.
2 ◆ Heat the oil in a large heatproof dish or paella pan and lightly fry the onion until brown. Stir in the rice, stock, wine and strained saffron liquid. Bring to the boil, stirring occasionally.
3 ◆ Stir in the peppers, tomatoes, garlic, herbs and seasoning, reduce the heat and simmer for 10 min, stirring occasionally.
4 ◆ Skin the haddock and cut into 5cm/2in pieces. Carefully add to the dish, cover with a tight-fitting lid and continue to cook for a further 10 min.
5 ◆ Stir in the mussels and peeled prawns and continue to simmer until the rice is quite tender and the liquid is absorbed.
6 ◆ Serve straight from the pan, garnished with whole prawns and sprigs of thyme, and accompanied with fresh crusty bread.

good pinch saffron
boiling water
45ml/3tbsp/4tbsp olive oil
1 large onion, finely chopped
225g/8oz long grain white rice
275ml/½pt/1¼ cups light stock
150ml/¼pt/⅔ cup dry white wine
½ yellow pepper, diced
½ green pepper, diced
225ml/½lb tomatoes, quartered
1 clove garlic, crushed
15ml/1tbsp chopped thyme
salt and freshly ground black pepper
350g/12oz fresh haddock fillet
100-150g/4-5oz cooked shelled mussels, canned or frozen
100-150g/4-5oz peeled prawns
whole prawns and sprigs thyme for garnish

SMOKED HADDOCK AND LIMA BEAN SALAD
Serves 2

1 ◆ Put the haddock in a saucepan and pour on sufficient milk and water to cover. Bring to the boil, cover and simmer for about 5 min, or until tender.
2 ◆ Drain the fish, remove and discard the skin. Break the fish into large flakes. Drain the lima beans and add to the fish.
3 ◆ Mix together the soured cream, curry paste, lemon juice and parsley. Season to taste and lightly fold the dressing into the haddock mixture.
4 ◆ Serve on a bed of salad leaves. Garnish the dish with hard-boiled egg (sieve the yolk and finely slice the white), freshly ground pepper and herbs. Serve with crusty bread.

350-450g/12-16oz smoked haddock fillet, skinned
a little milk and water
439g/15½oz can lima beans (or borlotti beans)
150ml/¼pt/⅔ cup soured cream
5-10ml/1-2tsp curry paste
45-60ml/3-4tbsp/4-5tbsp lemon juice
45ml/3tbsp/4tbsp chopped parsley
salt and freshly ground black pepper
mixed salad leaves
1-2 eggs, hard-boiled
fresh herbs and chicory to garnish
crusty bread for serving

POUSSINS WITH TARRAGON SAUCE
Serves 2

1 ◆ Place the poussins into a dish which is just large enough to hold them snugly.
2 ◆ Mix the lemon rind and juice and oil together, and season well with salt and pepper. Pour over the poussins in the dish. Cover and leave to marinate for at least 2 hr, or longer if you have the time. Turn them over occasionally.
3 ◆ Transfer to a roasting tin and cook in a preheated oven, 200°C/gas 6 for 40 min. Transfer to a preheated serving dish and keep warm. Reserve 30ml/2tbsp/3tbsp of the juices from the roasting tin.
4 ◆ Meanwhile, melt the butter in a small saucepan, add the spring onion and cook for 1-2 min. Stir in flour and cook for 1 min, stirring.
5 ◆ Gradually blend in the milk, reserved juices and the lemon juice. Add the tarragon, bring to the boil, stirring constantly then simmer gently for 5 min.
6 ◆ Stir the cream into the sauce, adjust seasoning to taste and spoon over or around the poussins.
7 ◆ Serve garnished with tarragon sprigs, finely sliced spring onion and lime twists.

2 poussins (approx 350g/12oz each)
1/2 lemon, juice and grated rind
45ml/3tbsp/4tbsp olive oil
15g/1/2oz butter
30ml/2tbsp/3tbsp finely sliced spring onion
15g/1/2oz plain flour (all-purpose flour)
150ml/1/4pt/2/3 cup milk
15ml/1tbsp lemon juice
10ml/2tsp chopped tarragon
tarragon sprigs, finely sliced spring onion and lime twists to garnish

ROAST CHICKEN WITH GARLIC
Serves 4-6

1 ◆ Remove the cloves of garlic from the bulb and leave them *unpeeled*.
2 ◆ Place garlic, olive oil, seasoning and herbs in the base of an earthenware dish.
3 ◆ Add the chicken to the dish, turning it in the oil and herbs to baste.
4 ◆ Make a thick paste with the flour and water and use to seal the lid to the earthenware dish.
5 ◆ Cook in a preheated oven at 190°C/gas 5 for 1½-1¾ hr. If not quite cooked when the lid is removed, replace in the oven and cook for a further 15-20 min.

2 bulbs of garlic
150ml/1/4pt/2/3 cup olive oil
salt and freshly ground black pepper
sprigs rosemary, thyme and sage
1½kg/3½lb chicken
50g/2oz plain flour
water

(*From top*) Poussin with Tarragon Sauce; Smoked Haddock and Lima Bean Salad

SPAGHETTI WITH HUMMUS SAUCE
Serves 2–3

225g/8oz green dried spaghetti
30ml/2tbsp/3tbsp oil
25g/1oz butter
100-150g/4-5oz mushrooms,
 finely chopped
1 bunch spring onions, sliced
225g/8oz hummus
30ml/2tbsp/3tbsp milk
salt, pepper and paprika
black or green olives for garnish
mixed salad leaves or fresh cooked
 broccoli for serving

Although hummus can be bought at most good supermarkets, try the easy recipe for Chickpea and Sesame Dip on page 16.

1 • Cook the spaghetti in plenty of salted water with a teaspoon of the oil until just tender, about 10 min. Drain well.
2 • Meanwhile, heat the rest of the oil with the butter and gently sauté the mushrooms and spring onions for a few minutes until softened.
3 • Stir in the hummus and milk with seasoning and paprika to taste, cover and simmer gently for 5-8 min.
4 • Combine the spaghetti with the sauce and toss well. Garnish with a few olives and serve with a salad or vegetables.

STEAK AND MUSHROOM PUFF PIE WITH RED WINE AND SESAME SEEDS
Serves 6

for the filling:
2 x 450g/1lb cans best quality
 cooked chunky steak
275g/10oz small button
 mushrooms
150ml/¹/4pt/²/3 cup red wine
15ml/1tbsp chopped thyme
30ml/2tbsp/3tbsp chopped
 parsley
1 bay leaf
5ml/1tsp made mustard
1-2 small cloves garlic, crushed

for the pastry topping:
375g/13oz ready-prepared frozen
 or chilled puff pastry
beaten egg to glaze
15g/¹/2oz sesame seeds for
 sprinkling

This is very easy to make using the very best quality canned cooked steak and ready-prepared pastry.

1 • Preheat the oven to 200°C/gas 6.
2 • Mix together all the ingredients for the filling and place into a 1½ litre/3pt/7½ cup pie dish fitted with a pie funnel if liked.
3 • Roll out the pastry thinly on a floured board and use to cover the pie in the usual way. Knock up the edges and make a small hole in the top of the pie. Roll out the trimmings to make pastry leaves to decorate the top if liked.
4 • Brush the pastry liberally with beaten egg and sprinkle generously with the sesame seeds.
5 • Bake towards the top of the oven for 25-30 min until the pastry is well risen, browned and crisp.

ROGAN JOSH
Serves 4

Tender cubes of meat or chicken in a rich sauce made with lentils and, for quickness, curry paste which gives a more authentic flavour than powder. Serve with rice, poppadums and chutney.

1 ♦ Place the meat or chicken in a bowl with the lemon juice and leave to marinate for about 30 min.
2 ♦ Meanwhile, heat the oil and gently sauté the onions until softened. Stir in the meat or chicken and fry briskly for 2-3 min.
3 ♦ Stir in the lemon rind, garlic, tomatoes, stock and lentils. Bring to the boil then cover the pan, lower the heat and simmer gently for about 1 hr until the lentils are cooked and the meat or chicken is tender.
4 ♦ Garnish with coriander and lemon wedges and serve hot.

675g/1¹/₂lb lean pork or lamb
  or chicken, diced
1 lemon, grated rind and juice
30ml/2tbsp/3tbsp oil
2 onions, sliced
25-30ml/1¹/₂-2tbsp/2-3tbsp
  curry paste
2-3 cloves garlic, crushed
450g/1lb tomatoes, skinned and
  chopped
150ml/¹/₄pt/²/₃ cup rich chicken
  stock
75g/3oz split red lentils
fresh coriander and lemon wedges
  to garnish

STIR-FRIED CHICKEN AND CASHEW NUTS
Serves 4

1 ♦ Cut the chicken into shreds and place in a bowl with the ginger and garlic. Cover and leave to stand.
2 ♦ Mix together the cornflour (cornstarch) with the soy sauce, sherry and chicken stock and set to one side.
3 ♦ Heat the oil in a wok or large pan and fry the cashews until lightly brown, stirring all the time. Remove them with a slotted spoon.
4 ♦ Add the chicken, ginger and garlic to the pan and stir-fry for 4-5 min, or until the chicken is cooked.
5 ♦ Stir the soy sauce mixture and then add to the pan. Keep stirring until blended and thickened, adding a little extra stock or water if it seems too thick. Adjust the seasoning.
6 ♦ Transfer to a hot serving dish and sprinkle with the cashews and sliced spring onions. Garnish with extra spring onions if liked and serve straight away.

450g/1lb boneless chicken
  breasts, skinned
2.5cm/1in piece fresh ginger,
  finely sliced
2 cloves garlic, finely sliced
10ml/2tsp cornflour (cornstarch)
15ml/1tbsp soy sauce
15ml/1tbsp dry sherry
150ml/¹/₄pt/²/₃ cup chicken stock
30ml/2tbsp/3tbsp oil
75g/3oz cashew nuts
salt and freshly ground black
  pepper
3 spring onions, finely sliced
spring onions, for garnish, optional

SWEET AND SOUR PORK
Serves 2

225g/8oz pork tenderloin
75-100g/3-4oz bean sprouts
15ml/1tbsp sherry
5ml/1tsp soy sauce
10ml/2tsp oil
4 spring onions, cut into
  2.5cm/1in lengths
1/2 red pepper, cut into strips
30ml/2tbsp/3tbsp cornflour
  (cornstarch)
150ml/1/4pt/2/3 cup water
10ml/2tsp tomato purée
10ml/2tsp light brown sugar
15ml/1tbsp wine vinegar
salt and freshly ground black
  pepper
1 small egg white
oil for deep-frying
buttered noodles or rice for serving

1 • Cut the pork into 5cm/2in strips and place in a bowl. Mix the sherry and soy sauce and pour over the pork. Leave to marinate for 1-2 hr.
2 • For the sauce, heat the oil in a pan, add the spring onion and red pepper and fry for 3-4 min, until soft. Gradually blend in 10ml/2tsp of cornflour (cornstarch) with the water, tomato purée, sugar, wine vinegar and seasoning. Stirring, bring to the boil and then remove from the heat.
3 • Drain the pork from the marinade and set aside. Add the marinade to the sauce.
4 • Separately, mix the egg white and the rest of the cornflour (cornstarch) together. Dip the pork into the mix and then deep-fry in hot oil for about 3 min, until golden. Drain on kitchen paper (paper towels).
5 • Stir the pork and bean sprouts into the sauce and simmer for 2 min. Serve with buttered noodles or boiled rice.

SWEET AND SOUR DUCK
Serves 4

4 small duck portions
60ml/4tbsp/5tbsp soy sauce
30ml/2tbsp/3tbsp brown sugar
45ml/3tbsp/4tbsp wine or cider
  vinegar
30ml/2tbsp/3tbsp dry sherry
juice of 1 orange
150ml/1/4pt/2/3 cup water
1.25ml/1/2tsp ground dry ginger
salt and freshly ground black
  pepper

1 • Roast the duck portions on a rack in a preheated oven at 190°C/gas 5 for 40-45 min, until the juices run clear and skin is crisp.
2 • Combine the remaining ingredients and bring to the boil. Simmer for 5-10 min, stirring continuously.
3 • Trim the duck joints if necessary and arrange on a serving platter. Coat with some of the sauce and hand the rest separately.

(*From top*) Rogan Josh; Stir -fried Chicken and Cashew Nuts; Sweet and Sour Pork

SPICED BEEF
Serves 6–8

900g/2lb fillet beef, trimmed
10ml/2tsp coarsely ground black
  peppercorns
75ml/3fl oz/¹/3 cup oil
1 clove garlic, crushed
2.5ml/¹/2tsp salt
5ml/1tsp dry mustard powder
5ml/1tsp ground ginger
30ml/2tbsp/3tbsp wholegrain
  mustard
15ml/1tbsp soft brown sugar

*This makes an ideal cold dish for summer entertaining.
Serve with a mixed leaf salad and herb sauce.*

1 • Tie the beef into a compact shape with string at about 2.5cm/1in intervals. Place the joint into a non-metallic dish.
2 • Mix the remaining ingredients together and spread over the beef. Cover the dish with a tight-fitting lid and leave to marinate overnight in the refrigerator.
3 • Preheat the oven to 240°C/gas 9. Transfer the beef to a small roasting dish and cook for 20 min. Reduce to 220°C/gas 7 for a further 20 min for a medium or 25 min for a well done result.
4 • Remove the meat from the oven, reserving the juices for the sauce (below). Leave to cool, then chill. When ready to serve, cut the meat into very thin slices and serve accompanied with the herb sauce.

HERB SAUCE

200ml/7fl. oz/1 cup olive oil
45ml/3tbsp/4tbsp lemon juice
30ml/2tbsp/3tbsp each chopped
  parsley, thyme and marjoram or
  basil
few drops tabasco
reserved pan juices from the meat
  (above)
salt and freshly ground black
  pepper

1 • Blend together the oil, lemon juice and herbs in a food processor or blender. Add a few drops of tabasco to taste.
2 • Skim any fat from the meat juices and blend into the sauce with salt and pepper. Adjust the seasoning and serve separately with the spiced beef.

LEMON AND WALNUT TURKEY
Serves 3–4

1 ♦ Dip the turkey fillets in the seasoned flour, then sauté in the butter until tender and browned.
2 ♦ Reserve three slices of lemon, and squeeze the remaining juice over the turkey. Sprinkle with thyme.
3 ♦ Cook for a few minutes longer, remove the turkey and cut into slices.
4 ♦ Return the turkey to the pan and sprinkle with the walnuts.
5 ♦ Serve straight from the pan with soured cream (sour cream) handed separately if liked.

*2 turkey breast fillets
  (approx 450g/1lb)
15ml/1tbsp/2tbsp seasoned flour
50g/2oz butter
1 lemon
15ml/1tbsp/2tbsp chopped thyme
25g/1oz chopped walnuts
soured cream (sour cream) for
  serving, optional*

MONKFISH WITH GARLIC AND TOMATOES
Serves 4

This easy way of stewing fish in a light tomato sauce can be adapted simply by varying the type of fish and variety of fresh herbs. Halibut, cod or hake or a mixture of fish can be simmered whole, as steaks or cutlets, or cut into pieces. Try the addition of fennel, thyme, rosemary, oregano, basil or marjoram.

1 ♦ Gently sauté the garlic in the olive oil in a large fry-pan. Add the tomatoes and salt and pepper and cook until just softened, about 3 min.
2 ♦ Add the monkfish and the bay leaf and sprinkle with the parsley. Cover and simmer gently for 10-15 min or until the fish is just cooked.
3 ♦ Remove the bay leaf, garnish with a few grapes if liked, and serve straight from the pan with crusty bread or fresh cooked spaghetti.

*2 cloves garlic, finely chopped
45-60ml/3-4tbsp/4-5tbsp olive
  oil
4 large tomatoes, skinned
  deseeded and chopped
salt and freshly ground black
  pepper
1kg/2lb monkfish
1 bay leaf
15-30ml/1-2tbsp/1-3tbsp
  chopped parsley
few grapes for garnish
crusty bread or spaghetti for serving*

PARTRIDGE IN A PAPER CASE
Serves 2

1 ♦ Melt the butter in a large fry-pan and gently sauté the two pieces of partridge for about 10 min. Remove them from the pan and sprinkle with salt, pepper, herbs and orange or lemon rind. Leave them to cool.
2 ♦ Prepare two oval pieces of greaseproof paper (wax paper) large enough to wrap each half bird and brush with melted butter or oil. Lay a bacon rasher centrally on each paper and the partridge halves on top.
3 ♦ Fold the paper over the half birds so that the edges of the paper are together and on top. Then fold about 1.25cm/½in around the edge over twice, to form a 'seam', crimping the edges to hold in position – like a Cornish pasty shape – so that the packages are airtight.
4 ♦ Put the parcels directly on an oven shelf and cook at 190°C/gas 5 for about 20-30 min until the partridge is tender.
5 ♦ Serve the parcels on hot plates as they are, with some orange or lemon for garnish.

5g/1oz butter
1 young partridge, cut into half lengthways
salt and freshly ground black pepper
15ml/1tbsp finely chopped fresh mixed herbs
5ml/1tsp finely grated orange or lemon rind
greaseproof paper (wax paper)
butter or oil for brushing
2 lean bacon rashers, derinded
orange or lemon for garnish, optional

LAMB WITH MINT AND REDCURRANT GLAZE
Serves 4

1 ♦ Heat the oil in a shallow fry-pan or sauté-pan and brown the lamb for a few minutes on each side.
2 ♦ Blend the redcurrant jelly and cornflour with the mint and stock, and pour into the pan. Add seasoning to taste.
3 ♦ Bring to the boil, then simmer without the lid for 10-15 min until the stock is reduced and syrupy.
4 ♦ Serve straight from the pan, garnished with mint.

15ml/1tbsp oil
4 medium or 8 small prime chump lamb steaks, trimmed of fat
45ml/3tbsp/4tbsp redcurrant jelly
15ml/1tbsp cornflour
15ml/tbsp fresh chopped mint
275ml/¹/2pt/1¹/2 cups lamb or chicken stock
salt and freshly ground black pepper
sprigs of mint to garnish

(*From top*) Partridge in a Paper Case; Monkfish with Garlic and Tomatoes

CRAB-STUFFED AUBERGINES
Serves 4

2 medium-size aubergines
salt
30ml/2tbsp/3tbsp oil
2 onions, sliced
15ml/1tbsp/2tbsp tomato purée
15m/1tbsp/2tbsp dried oregano
  or basil
225g/8oz crab meat (or tuna)
30ml/2tbsp/3tbsp fresh brown
  breadcrumbs
30ml/2tbsp/3tbsp grated
  parmesan cheese
30ml/2tbsp/3tbsp grated gruyère
  cheese
slivers butter

1 ♦ Cut the aubergines in half lengthways. Score the flesh with a knife, sprinkle with salt and leave to stand for 30 min. Rinse well and wipe dry.
2 ♦ Place aubergines on a baking sheet and cook at 180°C/gas 4 for 10-15 min until tender.
3 ♦ Heat the oil in a fry-pan, add the onions and cook until soft. Add the tomato purée, herbs, crabmeat and breadcrumbs. Mix well together.
4 ♦ Scoop the flesh from the cooked aubergines and chop finely. Add to the crab mixture and mix well.
5 ♦ Pile the mixture into the aubergine shells, sprinkle with the mixed grated cheeses and top with slivers of butter.
6 ♦ Place onto the baking tray and bake for a further 20-25 min. Serve hot or cold with bulghur and mint salad (page 153).

BULGHUR AND MINT SALAD
Serves 4

100g/4oz bulghur wheat
225ml/8fl oz/1 cup warm water
3 large sticks celery
1/4 cucumber
15-30ml/1-2tbsp/2-3tbsp olive
  oil
15ml/1tbsp finely chopped mint
  or 10ml/2tsp mint sauce
1 clove garlic, crushed
15-30ml/1-2tbsp/2-3tbsp
  lemon juice
salt and freshly ground black
  pepper
50g/2oz walnuts, coarsely
  chopped

1 ♦ Place the bulghur wheat into a bowl and pour on the warm water. Stir well, then leave for about 20 min until all the water has been absorbed.
2 ♦ Meanwhile, slice the celery finely, cut the cucumber into small dice and mix with all the remaining ingredients.
3 ♦ Stir the bulghur into the dish and adjust seasoning to taste. Cover the dish and leave to stand for 30 min, if time allows, to let the flavours develop.

Beef and Walnut Burgers
Serves 4–6

1 ◆ Sauté the onions in the butter until soft.
2 ◆ Mix together onion, tomatoes, meat, walnuts and seasoning.
3 ◆ Add sufficient egg to bind mixture together.
4 ◆ Shape into individual burgers and grill 6-8 min each side until firm and well browned.
5 ◆ Serve hot with jacket potatoes and coleslaw.

25g/1oz butter
2 medium onions, finely chopped
675g/1¹/₂lb lean braising steak, minced
75g/3oz chopped walnuts
5ml/1tsp paprika
seasoning
1-2 eggs beaten, to bind
2 tomatoes, skinned and chopped

Turkey and Avocado Stroganoff
Serves 2

1 ◆ Heat butter and oil in a fry-pan, add the onion and sauté until transparent.
2 ◆ Add salt and pepper to the flour and use to coat the turkey strips. Add to the pan and cook until the turkey has lost its pinkiness, tossing the strips and shaking the pan as necessary.
3 ◆ Stir the wine into the pan and cook for a further 5 min until the turkey is cooked. Remove the turkey with a draining spoon to a hot serving dish and keep warm.
4 ◆ Drain off all but 15ml/1tbsp of the juices from the pan, stir in the soured cream and beat in the mustard. Adjust the seasoning and heat gently.
5 ◆ Meanwhile, halve and stone the avocado. Scoop out the flesh and cut into thin slices.
6 ◆ Stir the turkey and sliced avocado into the soured cream and heat gently for a couple of minutes. Serve with tagliatelle.

15g/¹/₂oz butter
15ml/1tbsp oil
1 small onion, finely chopped
salt and freshly ground black pepper
5ml/1tsp flour
225g/8oz turkey breast slices, cut into narrow strips
30ml/2tbsp/3tbsp dry white wine
5-10ml/1-2tsp French mustard
65ml/2¹/₂fl oz/¹/₃ cup soured cream
1 ripe avocado
tagliatelle for serving

AUBERGINE STEW
Serves 4-6

675g/1¹/2lb aubergines
oil for shallow frying
675g/1¹/2lb tomatoes, skinned
  and chopped
¹/2 bottle red wine
salt and freshly ground black
  pepper
5-10ml/1-2tsp caster sugar, to
  taste
1-2 cloves garlic, finely chopped
15ml/1tbsp chopped thyme
1 bay leaf
15ml/1tbsp finely chopped parsley

This dish is as good cold as hot which enables it to be served in a variety of ways – as a starter or side dish as well as a main course.

1 • Cut the aubergines in half lengthways then into thick slices. Fry the slices a few at a time in oil over a high heat until lightly brown on both sides. Remove them from the pan and drain well on kitchen paper towel.
2 • Add the tomatoes to the pan with the wine, seasoning, sugar, garlic and bay leaf. Bring the mixture to the boil then simmer for 20 min.
3 • Add the aubergines to the pan, cover and simmer over a low heat for a further 30 min, adding a little water to moisten if necessary.
4 • Stir the parsley into the pan towards the end of cooking. Serve hot or cold.

FILLET STEAK WITH ROQUEFORT
Serves 4

25g/1oz butter
4 fillet steaks, about
  175-200g/6-7oz each
150ml/5fl oz/²/3 cup brandy
100g/4oz Roquefort cheese,
  crumbled
275ml/¹/2pt/1¹/4 cups crème
  fraîche or double cream (heavy
  cream)
salt and freshly ground black
  pepper
puréed potatoes and a green leaf
  salad for serving, optional

1 • Heat the butter in a fry-pan and cook the steaks briskly for 3-4 min each side, according to your preference.
2 • Pour the brandy into the pan and flame then transfer to a hot serving dish and keep warm.
3 • Add the Roquefort to the pan, stir in the cream and continue to cook gently to allow the sauce to thicken and become slightly syrupy. Season to taste.
4 • Spoon the sauce over the steaks and serve with puréed potatoes and a green leaf salad if liked.

(From top) Aubergine Stew; Turkey and Avocado Stroganoff; Fillet Steak with Roquefort

CASHEW AND WALNUT CUTLETS
Serves 4

150g/5oz cashew nuts, finely
  chopped
75g/3oz walnuts, finely chopped
50g/2oz wholewheat breadcrumbs
1 small onion, finely chopped
15ml/1tbsp/2tbsp chopped parsley
salt and freshly ground pepper
2.5ml/^{1}/2tsp each turmeric and
  allspice
5ml/1tsp ground cumin
1 large egg, beaten
oil for frying

1 • Place all the ingredients except the oil in a bowl and mix well together.
2 • Divide the mixture into 8 and shape each piece into a round or wedge. Cover and chill in the refrigerator for at least 1 hr.
3 • Lightly fry the cutlets in shallow oil for 2^1/2 min, turn them over and cook for a further 1^1/2-2 min on the second side.
4 • Serve hot or cold with a tossed salad and crusty bread.

CHICKEN LENTIL CURRY
Serves 4

4 chicken joints, skinned
175g/6oz orange lentils, washed,
  soaked and drained
2 onions, chopped
1 x 411g/14^1/2oz can tomatoes
2 potatoes, sliced
2.5ml/^{1}/2tsp chilli powder
5ml/1tsp turmeric
15ml/1tbsp/2tbsp coriander
5ml/1tsp cumin seeds
150-275ml/^{1}/4-^{1}/2pt/^{2}/3-1^1/4
  cups chicken stock
salt
lemon juice
25g/1oz butter

1 • Bring chicken, lentils, vegetables, spices and 150ml/^{1}/4pt/^{2}/3 cup stock to the boil. Cover and simmer for 30-45 min until the chicken is cooked and liquid absorbed.
2 • Remove the chicken, cut into bite-sized pieces.
3 • Purée the lentils and vegetables in a blender or food processor.
4 • Combine the chicken, lentil mixture, salt, lemon juice and butter. Heat through gently. Add more stock if necessary. (The sauce should just cover the chicken pieces.)
5 • Serve with plain rice, mango chutney and natural yoghurt.

LAMB IN CREAM AND ALMOND CURRY SAUCE
Serves 4–6

1 ⋅ Blend or crush the garlic, ginger, almonds and water to a paste.
2 ⋅ Heat the oil in a sauté- or fry-pan, brown the meat, then remove with a slotted spoon.
3 ⋅ Put the cardamom, cloves and nutmeg into the hot oil. Cook for 1-2 min. Add the onion and fry until browned.
4 ⋅ Add the paste, coriander, cumin and cayenne. Fry for 2-3 min, then add the meat, salt, cream and water.
5 ⋅ Bring to boil, cover and simmer for 1 hr. Remove the whole spices before serving with rye with raisins, if liked.

8 cloves garlic, peeled
2.5cm/1in cube fresh ginger, peeled and chopped
or 1.25ml/¼tsp ground ginger
50g/2oz almonds, blanched
150ml/¼pt/⅔ cup water
vegetable oil
1kg/2lb boned lamb (shoulder or leg), cut into 2.5cm/1in cubes
10 whole cardamom pods
6 whole cloves
stick cinnamon
225g/8oz onions, finely chopped
5ml/1tsp coriander seeds
10ml/2tsp cumin seeds
2.5ml/½tsp cayenne pepper
5ml/1tsp salt
275ml/½pt/1¼ cups single cream (light cream)
150ml/¼pt/⅔ cup water

RYE WITH RAISINS
Serves 4–6

1 ⋅ Place the rye groats or grain, raisins, bacon and salt in a large saucepan. Stir in the vegetable stock and mix well.
2 ⋅ Cover and simmer for 30-40 min until the rye is soft, stirring once or twice during the cooking time.
3 ⋅ Allow to stand for 5 min before serving as an alternative to rice.

225g/8oz rye groats or grain
75g/3oz raisins
50g/2oz bacon, de-rinded and sliced
2.5ml/½tsp salt
550ml/1pt boiling vegetable stock

1 bream, about 1kg/2lb
15-30ml/1-2tbsp/1-3tbsp olive
oil
juice 1/2 lemon
2 cloves garlic, chopped, optional
15ml/1tbsp chopped parsley
45-60ml/3-4tbsp/4-5tbsp dry
white wine
15-25ml/1-1 1/2tbsp/1-2tbsp
chopped parsley
15ml/1tbsp finely chopped or
minced (ground) onion
30-45ml/2-3tbsp/3-4tbsp fresh
breadcrumbs
salt and freshly ground black
pepper
lime slices and parsley for garnish
crusty bread and a salad for
serving

BAKED BREAM
Serves 2–3

Good fresh fish simply cooked and served is so reminiscent of Mediterranean summer holidays. Some crusty bread or plain boiled potatoes and a side salad is all that is needed to accompany the fish.

1 ⬩ Clean the fish well, rinse, dry and place in an earthenware oven dish. Brush the oil over the fish and sprinkle with the lemon juice and garlic.
2 ⬩ Pour the wine into the dish. Mix together the parsley, onion, breadcrumbs and seasoning and sprinkle over the top of the fish.
3 ⬩ Bake in a preheated oven at 200°C/gas 6 for 30-35 min or until the fish is cooked and the topping browned. Garnish with slices of lime and parsley and serve straight away.

HALIBUT STEAKS WITH FRENCH BEAN PURÉE
Serves 4

4 x 175-200g/6-7oz halibut
steaks
40g/1 1/2oz butter
1 lemon, grated rind and juice
350-400g/12-14oz cooked
French beans
15g/1/2oz fresh savory or parsley
salt and freshly ground black
pepper
lemon slices and herbs for garnish
boiled potatoes for serving

The basic recipe for the French bean purée can be used for almost any cooked vegetables.

1 ⬩ Melt about half of the butter and use to brush the halibut steaks. Sprinkle the fish with a few drops of the lemon juice then cook slowly under a medium grill.
2 ⬩ In the meantime, purée the French beans with a little savory or parsley in the processor or blender until smooth but still with a texture.
3 ⬩ Heat the remaining butter in a saucepan until beginning to brown.
4 ⬩ Stir in the lemon rind and rest of the juice and immediately add the purée of beans, stirring well. Season to taste.
5 ⬩ Serve the halibut with the purée in separate small dishes or ramekins. Garnish with lemon slices, a snip or two of herbs and serve with plain boiled potatoes.

(*From top*) Baked Bream; Halibut Steaks with French Bean Purée

PRAWNS THERMIDOR
Serves 3–4

450g/1lb peeled prawns
50g/2oz butter
15ml/1tbsp/2tbsp chopped onion
30ml/2tbsp/3tbsp chopped
 parsley
15-30ml/1-2tbsp/2-3tbsp
 chopped tarragon
25g/1oz flour
275ml/¹/2pt/1¹/4 cups milk
60ml/4tbsp/5tbsp white wine
pinch each mustard, salt,
 paprika
45ml/3tbsp/4tbsp grated
 parmesan cheese

1 ◆ Frozen prawns should be thawed and dried before use.
2 ◆ Melt 25g/1oz butter in a saucepan and add the onion, parsley, and tarragon. After a few minutes add the flour, then stir in the milk gradually.
3 ◆ Add the wine and seasonings. Simmer until reduced to a creamy consistency. Adjust seasoning to taste.
4 ◆ Add the prawns, seasoning, remaining butter and 30ml/2tbsp/3tbsp of the cheese.
5 ◆ Arrange the mixture in individual gratin dishes. Sprinkle with the remaining cheese and put under a hot grill to brown the top quickly. Serve at once.

LEMON SOLE WITH
MUSHROOMS AND YOGHURT
Serves 4–6

1kg/2lb lemon sole, filleted
50g/2oz seasoned flour
2 shallots, thinly sliced
225g/8oz button mushrooms,
 thinly sliced
100g/4oz butter
nutmeg, grated
seasoning
275ml/¹/2pt/1¹/4 cups Greek
 natural yoghurt

1 ◆ Cut the sole fillets into strips. Toss in the seasoned flour.
2 ◆ Fry thinly sliced shallots and button mushrooms in butter for 2-3 min or until tender. Add the fish and fry for a further 5-6 min.
3 ◆ Add the nutmeg and yoghurt and heat mixture through. Do not allow to boil. Adjust seasoning.
4 ◆ Garnish with chopped parsley and serve garnished with lemon twists.

COD ROMANA
Serves 4–6

1 • Remove the skin from the cod and cut the fish into 3.75cm/1½in pieces.
2 • Sprinkle the fish with salt and leave for 30 min to draw out some of the moisture. Rinse well in cold water, pat the pieces dry and toss in the seasoned flour.
3 • Heat 60ml/4tbsp/5tbsp oil in a fry-pan and lightly sauté the cod for about 8-10 min until tender.
4 • Drain well and remove the cod pieces from the dish. Add the remaining oil to the dish, stir in the onions and cook for 2 min. Add the peppers and cook until tender.
5 • Add the cod and tomatoes to the vegetables and mix carefully together. Season to taste and heat gently.
6 • Serve hot, sprinkled with chopped oregano or parsley.

675g/1½lb fresh cod fillet, thick end
salt for sprinkling
15ml/1tbsp/2tbsp seasoned flour
60-90ml/4-6tbsp/5-7tbsp oil
2 small onions, sliced
2 large green peppers, deseeded and sliced
1 × 539g/1lb 3oz can tomatoes, drained and quartered or
400g/1lb tomatoes, skinned and quartered
salt and freshly ground black pepper
15ml/1tbsp/2tbsp freshly chopped oregano or parsley for garnish

KING PRAWN AND PARMESAN RISOTTO
Serves 4-6

1 • Heat the oil and butter in a large, heavy-based fry-pan and fry the onion until tender.
2 • Add the wine and allow to bubble for a few minutes. Stir in the rice and stir over the heat for 2-3 min.
3 • Add the saffron to the stock and pour into the pan. Season to taste.
4 • Cook gently for 15-20 min, stirring frequently. Before the stock is completely absorbed, add the prawns and continue cooking for a further 5-10 min.
5 • Stir in most of the parmesan cheese and serve with the rest of the cheese handed separately.

15ml/1tbsp olive oil
25g/1oz butter
1 onion finely chopped
45-60ml/3-4tbsp/4-5tbsp dry white wine or vermouth
300-350g/10-12oz arborio (risotto) rice
good pinch saffron
1 litre/1¼pt/4½ cups fish, chicken or vegetable stock
salt and freshly ground black pepper
225-275g/8-10oz king prawns, peeled
100g/4oz fresh parmesan cheese, finely grated

Warm Duck Breast and Pine Kernel Salad
Serves 2

1 ♦ If liked, remove the duck skin and reserve to cook later.
2 ♦ Mix all ingredients for the marinade, pour over the duck breasts, cover and leave in the refrigerator to marinate 6-8 hr or overnight.
3 ♦ Remove the duck breasts from the marinade and pat dry with kitchen paper (paper towel). Slice the duck skin and cook under a medium grill until crisp.
4 ♦ Meanwhile, heat the oil in a pan until very hot and cook the duck for 2 min each side. Remove from the pan and fry the pine kernels until lightly brown.
5 ♦ Slice the duck breasts and return to the pan to heat through quickly.
6 ♦ Arrange salad on plates with French dressing. Top with slices of duck, pine kernels and crisp skin. Garnish with the orange wedges.

2 duck breasts
15-30ml/1-2tbsp/1-3tbsp olive oil
40g/1¹/₂oz pine kernels

for the marinade:
30ml/2tbsp/3tbsp sherry
30ml/2tbsp/3tbsp olive oil
15ml/1tbsp orange juice
5ml/1tsp salt
5ml/1tsp coriander
5ml/1tsp ginger
5ml/1tsp ground mace
1 clove garlic, crushed
mixed leaf salad tossed in hazelnut oil French dressing for serving
orange wedges for garnish

Beef and Mushroom Stroganoff
Serves 4–6

1 ♦ Cut the meat into strips 6x25mm/¹/₄x1in, toss in seasoned flour.
2 ♦ Fry thinly sliced onion and button mushrooms in the butter for 2-3 min until tender. Add the meat and fry for a further 5-6 min.
3 ♦ Add the nutmeg and soured cream (sour cream) or yoghurt and heat the mixture through. Do not allow to boil. Adjust the seasoning.
4 ♦ Garnish with chopped parsley and serve.

1kg/2lb rump or fillet steak
50g/2oz seasoned flour
2 small onions, thinly sliced
225g/8oz button mushrooms, thinly sliced
100g/4oz butter
nutmeg, grated
seasoning
275ml/¹/₂pt/1¹/₄ cups soured cream (sour cream) or natural yoghurt
chopped parsley for garnish

(*From top*) Venison Fillets with Port and Cream; Quail with Onions and Wine; Warm Duck Breast and Pine Kernel Salad

QUAIL WITH ONIONS AND WINE
Serves 4

8 quail, trussed
60ml/4tbsp/5tbsp olive oil
50g/2oz butter
4 slices bread, cut into round
  shapes
225g/8oz lean bacon, finely
  diced
12 small onions
salt and freshly ground black
  pepper
30-45ml/2-3tbsp/3-4tbsp
  wine
black olives or grapes and
  bay leaves for garnish

1 • Place the birds into a meat tin or ovenware dish and brush with some of the oil. Roast at 220°C/gas 7 for 20-25 min until brown and tender, basting once or twice.
2 • Meanwhile, heat the remaining oil with half the butter and fry the bread slices. Remove from the pan and keep warm.
3 • Add the remaining butter to the pan and fry the bacon with the onions until golden.
4 • Add the quail with the wine to the pan and cook for 5 more minutes. Place the quail on the fried bread and arrange the bacon and onion around. Garnish and serve.

VENISON FILLETS WITH PORT AND CREAM
Serves 4

45-60ml/3-4tbsp/4-5tbsp
  butter or oil
675-900g/1¹/2-2lb fillet of
  venison, cut into 8 slices
salt and freshly ground black
  pepper
30ml/2tbsp/3tbsp crème fraîche
  or double cream (heavy cream)
  or thick Greek yoghurt
60-75ml/4-5tbsp/5-6tbsp port
chopped parsley for garnish

1 • Heat the butter or oil in a fry-pan and sauté the venison slices for 4-5 min each side over a high heat until they are lightly browned.
2 • Remove the fillets from the pan and arrange on a hot serving platter. Sprinkle with salt and pepper and keep warm.
3 • Add the cream and port to the pan and stir to mix in the cooking juices. Heat gently, making sure the sauce does not boil. Adjust the seasoning.
4 • Pour the sauce over the venison, sprinkle with plenty of chopped parsley and serve straight away.

VEGETABLE CASSEROLE WITH SMOKED CHEESE
Serves 2

1 ◆ Heat the oil in a flameproof casserole, add garlic, onion and green pepper and sauté until the onion is soft, about 4 min. Set the oven to 190°C/gas 5.
2 ◆ Add the cauliflower, courgettes, sweetcorn, creamed tomato or passata, pearl barley, water, herbs and paprika to the dish and add seasoning to taste.
3 ◆ Bring to the boil and bubble for 1-2 min, stirring, then add the kidney beans.
4 ◆ Sprinkle with the breadcrumbs and the smoked cheese. Bake in the hot oven for 35-40 min until the vegetables are tender and the topping is golden brown.
5 ◆ Sprinkle with parsley and serve with crusty French bread or jacket potatoes topped with soured cream and chives.

15ml/1tbsp olive oil
1 clove garlic, crushed
1 small onion, chopped
1/2 green pepper, cut into strips
175g/6oz cauliflower florets
100g/4oz courgettes, sliced
50g/2oz sweetcorn kernels
175ml/6fl oz/3/4 cup creamed tomatoes or passata
50g/2oz pearl barley
90ml/6tbsp/8tbsp water
5ml/1tsp basil, chopped
15ml/1tbsp parsley, chopped
5ml/1tsp paprika
213g/7 1/2oz can red kidney beans, drained
salt and freshly ground black pepper
75-90ml/5-6tbsp/6-8tbsp fresh breadcrumbs
100g/4oz smoked cheese, grated
chopped parsley to garnish

TROUT WITH LEMON AND ALMONDS
Serves 2

1 ◆ Wash the trout and pat dry with kitchen paper (paper towel).
2 ◆ Sprinkle inside and out with lemon juice and season, then place in grill pan.
3 ◆ Sprinkle the trout with the almonds and cook under a medium/hot grill for 10-15 min.
4 ◆ Garnish with lemon slices as necessary and serve straight away with new potatoes and mixed salad.

2 medium trout
juice of 1 lemon
salt and freshly ground pepper
25g/1oz flaked almonds
thin slices of lemon for garnish
buttered new potatoes and salad for serving

DESSERTS

675-900g/1¹/2-2lb *fresh exotic
fruits to choice eg. pineapple,
pawpaw, mango, fresh figs,
grapes, kiwi fruits, kumquats,
Ogen or Charentais melon*

for the liqueur cream:
425ml/³/4pt/2 cups *whipping
cream*
60ml/4tbsp/5tbsp *icing sugar
(confectioner's sugar)*
2.5ml/¹/2tsp *vanilla essence
(vanilla extract)*
30ml/2tbsp/3tbsp *fruit flavoured
liqueur to choice eg. Grand
Marnier, Eau de Vie de Poires
William, Calvados*

75g/3oz *plain chocolate (bitter
chocolate)*
30ml/2tbsp/3tbsp *strong black
coffee*
2 eggs, *separated*
15ml/1tbsp *Tia Maria*
pinch cream of tartar
*chocolate curls or toasted chopped
hazelnuts and* 30ml/2tbsp/3tbsp
*whipped cream for decoration,
optional*

EXOTIC FRUIT BROCHETTES WITH LIQUEUR CREAM
Serves 6–8

1 ◆ Prepare the fruit into bite-size pieces and thread alternately on to thin bamboo skewers, reserving 6-8 pieces for decoration.
2 ◆ In a large cold bowl, beat the cream until in soft peaks, then add the rest of the ingredients and continue to beat until thick. Take care not to overbeat. Store in the refrigerator until ready to use.
3 ◆ Place a fruit brochette on to each serving plate with a good spoonful or two of the cream. Decorate with the reserved fruit.

CHOCOLATE MOCHA MOUSSE
Serves 2

The basic mousse recipe can be easily adapted. Replace the coffee and liqueur with orange juice and Grand Marnier or Cointreau, and a delicious orange mousse can be made.

1 ◆ Break the chocolate into small pieces and place into a bowl over a pan of simmering hot water until melted.
2 ◆ Stir in the black coffee. Allow the chocolate to cool slightly before mixing in the egg yolks and liqueur.
3 ◆ Whisk the egg whites with the cream of tartar until soft peaks form then fold a little into the chocolate to lighten the mixture, then gently fold in the rest until well blended.
4 ◆ Spoon or pour the mixture into two ramekins or dessert glasses and chill until set.
5 ◆ Decorate with chocolate curls or toasted chopped hazelnuts and whipped cream.

CHOCOLATE CURLS

Shave thin layers from a block of chocolate at room temperature with a potato peeler and chill until required.

(*Previous page, clockwise from left*) Exotic Fruit Brochettes with Liqueur Cream; Purées of Fruits; Chestnut Meringues; Chocolate Mocha Mousse

PURÉES OF FRUITS
Serves 4

A spectacular but simply prepared recipe which uses the fresh fruits of summer for a most refreshing dessert. When fresh fruits are not available, frozen, canned or dried fruit purées may be used instead.

1 ◆ For each serving, save one or two of the fruits for decoration. Stew the rest of the fruits separately in 30-45ml/2-3tbsp orange juice, dry white wine or water with a little sugar or honey to taste, until tender.

2 ◆ Drain off and reserve some of the juices then purée the fruits separately in a food processor or blender. Try to ensure that the purées are of similar consistencies, adding back some of the juices as necessary.

3 ◆ Sieve the purées if necessary to remove skins or pips then chill until ready for serving.

4 ◆ Place spoonsful of the purées alternately around individual serving plates and a spoonful or two of the whipped cream or yoghurt or fromage frais in the centres.

5 ◆ Gently shake the plates so that the purées just run together or carefully swirl them together with a fork.

6 ◆ Dust with sieved icing sugar (confectioner's sugar) if liked and decorate with the reserved fruit and mint leaves. Serve with ratafias or wafers if liked.

150-175g/5-6oz each of 4-5 fruits of different colours eg. raspberries, gooseberries, blackberries, apricots, peaches, redcurrants
a little orange juice, dry white wine or water
sugar or honey to taste, optional
60-75ml/4-5tbsp/5-6tbsp whipped cream, or yoghurt or fromage frais
icing sugar (confectioner's sugar) and mint leaves for decoration, optional
ratafias or wafers for serving, optional

CHESTNUT MERINGUES
Serves 4

1 ◆ Whip the cream until stiff. Break down the chestnut purée with a wooden spoon then beat until smooth.

2 ◆ Fold the whipped cream into the chestnut purée with the liqueur then pipe or spoon the mixture into the meringue nests.

3 ◆ Decorate with small pieces of marron glacé or some toasted flaked almonds. Serve straight away.

150ml/¹/4pt/²/3 cup double (heavy) or whipping cream
225g/8oz can sweetened chestnut purée
30ml/2tbsp/3tbsp Grand Marnier liqueur
8 ready-made meringue nests
small pieces of marron glacé or toasted flaked almonds to decorate

ICED KIWI FRUIT SABAYON
Serves 4

*4 large kiwi fruit, about
350g/12oz
100g/4oz icing sugar
(confectioner's sugar)
60ml/4tbsp/5tbsp water
1 lime, grated rind and juice
30ml/2tbsp/3tbsp Bacardi
4 egg yolks
225ml/8fl oz/1 cup whipping
cream
slices kiwi fruit for serving, optional*

1 ⬩ Peel the kiwi fruit and place in a saucepan with the icing sugar (confectioner's sugar) and water. Heat gently and simmer for 8-10 min until softened. Leave to cool slightly then purée in a food processor or blender.
2 ⬩ Stir the lime rind and juice into the purée with the Bacardi and leave to cool.
3 ⬩ Add 30ml/2tbsp/3tbsp of the mixture to the egg yolks and whisk vigorously until thick and mousse-like; gradually whisk in the rest of the mixture.
4 ⬩ Lightly whip the cream and fold into the kiwi mixture. Turn into a freezer container, cover, seal and freeze until firm, about 3 hr.
5 ⬩ When ready to serve, transfer to the refrigerator for about 10 min to soften. Serve scoops in stemmed glasses topped with a slice of kiwi fruit if liked.

ICED HONEY AND
ALMOND CREAM WITH AMARETTO
Serves 6

*50g/2oz flaked almonds, toasted
2 egg whites
75g/3oz clear honey (thin
honey), warmed
225ml/8fl. oz/1 cup whipping
cream, whipped
few drops almond essence
few drops vanilla essence (vanilla
extract)
90ml/6tbsp/8tbsp amaretto (or
other liqueur)*

Although easy to prepare, this dessert should be made in advance then frozen for 3 hr before serving.

1 ⬩ Reserve two-thirds of the toasted almonds for decoration and finely chop the rest.
2 ⬩ Whisk the egg whites until they hold soft peaks and gradually add the honey in a thin stream or a spoonful at a time. Beat until stiff and glossy.
3 ⬩ Carefully fold together the whisked egg whites, whipped cream, almond and vanilla essences and the chopped nuts until just blended.
4 ⬩ Spoon into 6 freezer-proof glasses, cover each with freezer plastic film and freeze for 3 hr.
5 ⬩ Serve with a tablespoon of amaretto on top of each serving and sprinkle with the reserved toasted almonds.

(*Clockwise from top left*) Iced Kiwi Fruit Sabayon; Mango Sorbet; Blackcurrant and Cassis Sorbet; Iced Honey and Almond Cream with Amaretto

BLACKCURRANT AND CASSIS SORBET
Serves 4–6

450g/1lb blackcurrants, fresh or
 frozen
175g/6oz caster sugar
275ml/¹/2pt/1¹/4 cups water
juice 1 lemon
30ml/2tbsp/3tbsp crème de
 cassis
mint leaves for garnish
crisp dessert biscuits for serving
 (page 108)

*Once the sorbet has been prepared, the scoops can be made well
ahead of time and returned to the freezer until required.*

1 • Remove fresh blackcurrants from their stalks, wash and dry the fruit. Thaw frozen blackcurrants. Purée the fruit in a food processor or blender then rub through a sieve to remove skin and pips.
2 • Place the sugar and water into a pan and heat gently, stirring to dissolve the sugar. Bring to the boil, simmer for 2 min then remove from the heat.
3 • Combine the syrup with the blackcurrant purée, lemon juice and crème de cassis. Leave to cool then chill. Transfer the chilled syrup to a shallow freezer container and freeze until hard – about 4 hr.
4 • Break up the ice and replace into the processor or blender with a steel blade. Process the mixture until quite smooth.
5 • Return the iced mixture to the freezer container, cover, seal and freeze again for several hours until firm.
6 • Transfer to the refrigerator for 20-25 min to soften before serving in scoops on individual plates or in serving glasses. Garnish with mint and serve with crisp dessert biscuits.

APPLE MINT WHIP
Serves 4–6

675g/1¹/2lb cooking apples,
 sliced
45ml/3tbsp/4tbsp clear honey
 (thin honey)
30ml/2tbsp/3tbsp water
6 large sprigs mint
150ml/¹/4pt/²/3 cup double
 (heavy) or whipping cream
2 egg whites
15ml/1tbsp sugar
crème de menthe for serving,
 optional

1 • Place the apples in a pan with the honey, water and mint, saving the tops of the sprigs for decoration. Cover and simmer for 10-15 min until tender. Leave to cool slightly then remove and discard the mint.
2 • Purée the apples in a food processor or blender then leave until cold.
3 • In separate bowls, whip the double or whipping cream (heavy cream) and the egg whites with the sugar.
4 • Gently fold the cream into the apples followed by the egg whites. Blend carefully until smooth.
5 • Spoon into individual glasses or dishes and chill. Serve drizzled with a little crème de menthe if liked and decorated with the reserved mint leaves.

MANGO SORBET
Serves 4

Choose ripe mangoes which are turning golden yellow to give the most delicious flavour to this refreshing sorbet.

100g/4oz caster sugar
350ml/12fl. oz/1¹/2 cups water
2 lemons, thinly pared rind and
 juice
2 very ripe mangoes
4 egg whites
good pinch cream of tartar
slices of mango for serving, optional

1 ◆ Place the sugar and water in a saucepan over a gentle heat and stir until the sugar has dissolved. Add the lemon rind and simmer for 10 min. Leave to cool.
2 ◆ Cut the mangoes in halves around the stones and scoop out all the flesh into a blender or food processor. Blend with the lemon juice until smooth.
3 ◆ Remove and discard the lemon rind from the syrup. Combine the syrup with the mango purée and when smooth, pour into a shallow freezer container. Freeze for 2-3 hr until half frozen and slushy, stirring occasionally.
4 ◆ Whisk the egg whites with the cream of tartar until soft peaks form then fold into the sorbet. Replace into the container, cover, seal and freeze until firm.
5 ◆ Transfer the sorbet to the refrigerator to soften about 15-20 min before required. Serve in scoops in individual dishes or dessert glasses or on plates with slices of fresh mango.

BANANAS WITH ORANGE
Serves 2

finely grated rind and juice of 1
 orange
15ml/1tbsp light soft brown sugar
5cm/2in piece cinnamon stick
2 bananas
15ml/1tbsp Grand Marnier or
 Cointreau
15g/¹/2oz desiccated coconut,
 toasted
ice-cream or yoghurt for serving

1 ◆ Place the orange rind and juice, sugar and cinnamon stick into a pan and heat gently until the sugar has dissolved, stirring occasionally.
2 ◆ Peel the bananas and cut each one lengthways and widthways and place into the pan with the orange juice. Swirl the pan to coat the bananas with the juices then cover and simmer for 4-5 min until just tender.
3 ◆ Transfer the bananas to a serving dish. Discard the cinnamon and add the liqueur to the syrup. Pour over the bananas and sprinkle with the coconut.
4 ◆ Serve warm or chilled with ice-cream or yoghurt.

BANANA AND KIWI FLANS
Serves 4

1 ◆ Combine the crushed biscuits with the melted butter and press into the base and around the sides of four 10cm/4in individual flan tins. Place into the freezer for a few minutes while preparing the filling.
2 ◆ Peel the bananas and purée in a food processor or blender with the lemon juice and icing sugar. Process until really smooth.
3 ◆ Whip the cream until just stiff and fold into the banana mixture. Divide between the chilled flan cases and smooth the tops.
4 ◆ Chill before serving decorated with the sliced kiwi fruit.

100g/4oz chocolate digestive biscuits (graham crackers), crushed
25g/1oz butter, melted
2 small bananas
20ml/4tsp lemon juice
15ml/1tbsp icing sugar (confectioner's sugar)
150ml/1/4pt/2/3 cup double (heavy) or whipping cream
1 kiwi fruit, thinly sliced for decoration

APRICOT CHEESE FLANS
Serves 4

Follow the recipe for the flan biscuit bases above. Set to chill in the freezer while making this alternative filling.

1 ◆ Pat the apricots dry with kitchen paper (paper towel). Save 2 apricot halves for decoration.
2 ◆ Blend the rest of the apricots in a food processor or blender with the cheese, cardamom and lemon juice to taste. Blend until smooth.
3 ◆ Pour the mixture into the chilled flan cases and chill again until the filling is firm.
4 ◆ Thinly slice the reserved apricots and use to decorate the tops of the flans. Sprinkle with pistachio nuts.

400g/14oz can apricot halves in natural juice, drained
100g/4oz full fat soft cheese
pinch ground cardamom
lemon juice
pistachio nuts

(*From top*) Banana and Kiwi Flan; French Apple Tartlets; Fresh Figs with Yoghurt Cream

FRESH FIGS WITH YOGHURT CREAM
Serves 4

8 fresh figs
150ml/¼pt/⅔ cup double
  cream, (heavy cream), lightly
  whipped
150ml/¼pt/⅔ cup natural
  yoghurt
45-60ml/3-4tbsp/4-5tbsp soft
  brown sugar
fresh fig or vine leaves to decorate,
  optional

This refreshing sweet may bring back memories of the Mediterranean table – especially if decorated with fresh fig or vine leaves.

1 • Place the figs in a large bowl and pour hot water over to cover. Leave to stand for about 1 min then drain. Peel off the skins and cut each fig into quarters.
2 • Gently fold the lightly whipped cream into the yoghurt and stir until blended.
3 • Spoon a little of the yoghurt cream into the bottom of 4 serving glasses and top with a layer of figs, followed by more cream, then figs, sprinkling each layer with brown sugar. Finish with a layer of cream and sugar on top.
4 • Chill in the refrigerator for at least 2 hr before serving, to let the sugar melt into the cream. Serve the glasses on plates decorated with fig or vine leaves if liked.

BAKED PEAR PUDDING
Serves 4–5

4-5 firm pears, peeled, cored and
  halved
15ml/1tbsp lemon juice
butter
165ml/5½fl oz/⅔-¾ cup milk
75ml/2½fl oz/⅓ cup single
  cream (light cream)
75g/3oz sugar
40g/1½oz plain flour (all-
  purpose flour)
2 eggs, size 1 (large)
2.5ml/½tsp vanilla essence
  (vanilla extract)
15ml/1tbsp caster sugar
5ml/1tsp ground cinnamon
25g/1oz unsalted butter
½ quantity liqueur cream made
  with Eau de Vie de Poires
  William (or similar) for serving

1 • Set the oven to preheat to 220°C/gas 7.
2 • Brush the pears with the lemon juice then slice each half lengthways or widthways and arrange slightly fanned out in one layer in a well buttered flan dish.
3 • Combine the milk, cream, sugar, flour, eggs and essence (extract) and whisk together to make a smooth batter. Pour over the pears.
4 • Mix the caster sugar and cinnamon together and sprinkle over the surface of the pears. Dot with the butter.
5 • Bake for about 15 min then reduce the heat to 180°C/gas 4 for a further 30-40 min until the batter has set and browned.
6 • Leave to cool a bit before serving warm with the liqueur cream to bring out the flavour.

FRENCH APPLE TARTLETS
Serves 4

The pastry tartlet cases may be made well ahead of time.

1 ∙ Preheat the oven to 200°C/gas 6.
2 ∙ Place the flour in a bowl, add the butter and rub into the flour until it resembles breadcrumbs. Stir in the almonds and sufficient egg to make a dough. Knead lightly then cover and chill for 30 min.
3 ∙ Roll out the dough on a floured surface and use to line four 9-10cm/3½-4in tartlet tins. Prick the bases well with a fork.
4 ∙ Line the pastry with circles of greaseproof paper (wax paper) and fill with ceramic or baking beans. Bake blind for 10 min, remove the beans and bake for a further 3-5 min to dry out.
5 ∙ Meanwhile, dip the apple slices in the lemon juice. Arrange the slices overlapping in circles in the pastry tartlets. Brush the tops liberally with the apricot jam to glaze.
6 ∙ Either brown the tartlets under a low to medium hot grill until lightly browned or return to the oven and bake until golden. Decorate with a small piece of strawberry if liked.

for the pastry:
175g/6oz plain flour (all-purpose flour)
75g/3oz butter, cut into small pieces
25g/1oz ground almonds
½-1 egg, beaten

for the filling:
4 small eating apples, sliced
30ml/2tbsp/3tbsp lemon juice
60-90ml/4-6tbsp/5-8tbsp apricot jam, sieved and warmed
1 strawberry for garnish, optional

GINGER SPICED PEACHES
Serves 2

Preserved ginger and cardamom are combined to give an unusual spicy tang to the peaches but other fruits such as pears or apricots could be used instead.

1 ∙ Place the peaches in a single layer into a small bowl or jug and pour over boiling water to cover. Leave for a couple of minutes, then drain and carefully peel off the skins.
2 ∙ Cut the peaches into halves around the stones and brush with lemon juice. Place into a saucepan with the rest of the lemon juice and the remaining ingredients. Simmer gently for about 12 min or until tender.
3 ∙ Using a draining spoon, transfer the peaches to a serving dish. Boil the syrup vigorously for 3 min, pour over the peaches and leave to cool.
4 ∙ Serve with yoghurt or ice-cream.

2 firm peaches
boiling water
juice ½ lemon
seeds from 4 cardamom pods
175ml/6fl oz/¾ cup water
4 pieces preserved stem ginger, thinly sliced
60ml/4tbsp/5tbsp preserved ginger syrup
yoghurt or ice-cream for serving

CHILLED CHERRY SOUP WITH ORANGE
Serves 4

1 orange
225g/8oz red or black cherries,
  stoned
75ml/5tbsp/6tbsp dry white
  wine
350g/12oz natural yoghurt,
  stirred
20ml/4tsp natural yoghurt for
  decoration
crisp dessert biscuits for serving
  (page 108)

The chilled fruit soup is traditionally from Hungary. This recipe uses cherries but strawberries or raspberries make ideal alternatives. It is best served well chilled.

1 ◆ Grate the rind from the orange and squeeze the juice. Reserve 4 cherries.
2 ◆ Place the orange juice with the rest of the cherries and wine in a food processor or blender and purée until very smooth. Stir in the yoghurt and grated orange rind then chill for at least 1 hr.
3 ◆ When ready to serve, pour the soup into 4 serving dishes. Add a teaspoon of yoghurt to the centre of each one and lightly swirl.
4 ◆ Decorate with the reserved cherries and serve with crisp dessert biscuits.

STRAWBERRY CHEESE WITH BLACK PEPPER
Serves 4–5

450g/1lb full fat soft cheese
100-150g/4-5oz strawberries,
  finely chopped
25-40ml/1^1/2-2^1/2tbsp/2-
  3^1/2tbsp crushed black (or green)
  peppercorns
extra strawberries, celery, cheese
  crackers and butter curls for
  serving

This recipe combines the cheese and dessert courses and makes a nice end to a summer dinner party. Green peppercorns, which are milder in flavour, can be used if preferred.

1 ◆ Beat the cream cheese until soft and carefully mix with the chopped strawberries.
2 ◆ Form into a round or sausage shape and wrap in greaseproof paper (wax paper) or plastic film. Chill for at least 1 hr.
3 ◆ When ready to serve, roll the cheese in the crushed peppercorns. Serve cut into slices with extra strawberries, celery, crackers and butter.

(*From top*) Chilled Cherry Soup with Orange; Walnut Thins; Potted Camembert with Walnuts; Strawberry Cheese with Black Pepper

LANGUES DE CHAT
Makes about 48

75g/3oz butter, softened
75g/3oz caster sugar
few drops vanilla essence (vanilla
    extract)
2 egg whites
75g/3oz plain flour (all-purpose
    flour)

*These traditional biscuits can be finished in
different ways to add variety.*

1 • Preheat the oven to 200°C/gas 6 and grease or oil 2 baking trays.
2 • In a large bowl, beat together the butter and sugar until light and creamy. Beat in the vanilla essence (vanilla extract).
3 • Lightly mix the egg whites and beat in about one-third to the creamed mixture. Beat in some of the flour, then another third of the egg whites, followed by more flour then the rest of the egg whites. Finally fold in the remaining flour.
4 • Spoon the mixture into a large piping bag fitted with a 1/2cm/1/4in plain nozzle. Pipe the mixture on to the prepared baking trays in lengths of about 6cm/2in leaving plenty of room to spread.
5 • Bake the first batch for 4-6 min or until the edges are tinged brown. Remove with a palate knife on to cooling trays. Repeat the piping and baking until all the mixture is used up.

CURLS AND TWISTS
Makes about 48

1 • While the biscuits are still soft from the oven, quickly ease them off the baking trays and twist around handles of wooden spoons.
2 • As soon as they have cooled and hardened, slide them off the handles on to cooling trays to be ready for the next batch from the oven.

ALMOND, WALNUT OR HAZELNUT THINS
Makes about 36

1 • When the mixture has been prepared (to the end of method 3), drop teaspoons of the mixture on to the greased baking trays, leaving plenty of space to spread.
2 • Place a few flaked almonds, or a sprinkling of finely chopped walnuts or hazelnuts on top of each one and bake for 6-8 min or until the edges have tinged brown.
3 • Remove to cooling trays and repeat until all the mixture is used. For a curved shape, place around a rolling pin to cool.

SERVING CUPS
Makes about 18

1 ⬩ To make the biscuits spread more thinly, add an extra 15g/½oz sugar to the recipe.
2 ⬩ At the end of method 3, drop only about 2 or 3 rounded teaspoons on to the greased baking trays to allow plenty of room to spread. With the tip of a spoon, gently spread the mixture out into rounds about 10cm/4in.
3 ⬩ Bake for 5-6 min or until tinged brown at the edges.
4 ⬩ Have ready 4 or 6 upturned cups. Carefully remove the biscuits from the baking trays with a fish-slice and form them over the bases of the upturned cups.
5 ⬩ Leave the biscuits to harden for a few minutes then remove them from the cups to cooling trays to be ready for the next batch from the oven.

POTTED CAMEMBERT WITH WALNUTS
Serves 4-6

1 ⬩ Blend the cheeses and butter together in a food processor or blender if available or use your hand initially to work the mixture then beat with a wooden spoon.
2 ⬩ When the mixture is thoroughly blended and creamy, combine with the walnuts and mix in the kirsch and pepper to taste.
3 ⬩ Divide into ramekins, smooth the tops and garnish each one with a walnut half. If you have the time, cover and chill in the refrigerator overnight if possible to allow the flavours to develop.
4 ⬩ Remove from the fridge 15-20 min to soften before serving with celery, fresh pears and a glass of port.

1 Camembert cheese, cut into small pieces
100g/4oz full fat soft cheese, softened
50g/2oz unsalted butter, softened
75g/3oz walnuts, roughly chopped
45ml/3tbsp/4tbsp kirsch (or Calvados or dry vermouth)
freshly ground black pepper
4-6 walnut halves for decoration
celery, fresh pears and a glass of port for serving

BREAD AND BUTTER PUDDING WITH RUM AND GINGER
Serves 5–6

1 ⬧ Layer the bread with the dried fruits and ginger in an ovenware dish, sprinkling each layer with sugar and finishing with some fruit, ginger and sugar on the top.
2 ⬧ Beat the eggs and gradually beat in the milk and cream with nutmeg to taste. Strain through a sieve into the dish over the bread and leave to soak for about 45 min.
3 ⬧ Preheat the oven to 180°C/gas 4. Sprinkle the top of the pudding with a little more nutmeg if liked, then bake for 25-35 min or until puffed and golden. Serve straight away, with cream if liked.

5 slices buttered bread
75g/3oz currants and sultanas mixed, soaked in dark rum (or orange juice)
15-30ml/1-2tbsp/1-3tbsp chopped crystallised ginger, to taste
25-50g/1-2oz demerara sugar (brown sugar), to taste
3 eggs
425ml/³/4pt/2 cups milk
150ml/¹/4pt/²/3 cup single cream (light cream)
grated nutmeg
cream for serving, optional

REDCURRANTS AND FROMAGE FRAIS
Serves 4

The season for redcurrants is not long but this simple recipe makes a light refreshing summer pudding. It can also be made with blackcurrants and thick Greek natural yoghurt.

1 ⬧ Mix together the fromage frais and the redcurrants and sweeten to taste with the honey or apple juice. Stir in the mint.
2 ⬧ Whisk the egg white until stiff but not dry and fold into the redcurrant mixture.
3 ⬧ Serve in individual glasses or dishes and decorate with mint leaves and redcurrants if liked.

275ml/¹/2pt/1¹/4 cups fromage frais
450g/1lb redcurrants, topped and tailed
honey or concentrated apple juice to taste
15ml/1tbsp chopped mint
1 egg white
few mint leaves and sprigs redcurrants for decoration, optional

(*From top*) Bread and Butter Pudding with Rum and Ginger;
Redcurrants and Fromage Frais; Treacle Tart

TREACLE TART
Serves 5–6

for the pastry:
*200g/7oz plain flour
(all-purpose flour)
pinch salt
150g/5oz butter, cut into small
pieces
1 egg yolk*

for the filling:
*5-6/6-8 rounded tbsp golden
syrup (light corn syrup)
3/4 rounded tbsp fresh white or
brown breadcrumbs
1/2 lemon, finely grated rind and
juice
cream for serving*

The traditional golden syrup (light corn syrup) lattice tart has been a favourite for many years.

1 • Preheat the oven to 200°C/gas 6.
2 • Place the flour and salt into a bowl, add the butter and rub into the flour until it resembles breadcrumbs.
3 • Using a fork, mix in the egg yolk and sufficient cold water to make a dough. Knead lightly.
4 • Roll out the dough on a floured surface and line a 20cm/8in pie plate. Lightly knead the trimmings, roll out and cut into thin strips.
5 • Mix the rest of the ingredients together and spread on to the pastry.
6 • Arrange the reserved strips of pastry in a lattice style over the top, dampen the edges and trim neatly.
7 • Bake for 25-30 min until golden brown. Serve warm or cold, drizzled with cream or whipped cream.

GREENGAGE CRUMBLE
Serves 4–6

*100g/4oz rolled oats
100g/4oz wholewheat flour
100g/4oz butter
50-75g/2-3oz soft brown sugar
675-900g/1 1/2-2lb greengages
(or plums or damsons), halved
and stoned
sugar to taste
cream, yoghurt or ice-cream for
serving*

For a special occasion, it is quite nice to serve the crumble in individual small dishes or ramekins.

1 • Preheat the oven to 200°C/gas 6.
2 • Place the oats and flour into a bowl. Cut the butter into small pieces and rub in. Stir in the sugar, keeping 15ml/1tbsp in reserve.
3 • Place the prepared fruit into an ovenware dish (or individual dishes) and sprinkle with sugar to taste. Sprinkle the crumble mixture evenly over the fruit and sprinkle the reserved sugar over the top.
4 • Cook the crumble in a preheated oven for 35-45 min until cooked and golden brown.
5 • Serve hot, warm or cold with cream, yoghurt or ice-cream.

GRAPE AND YOGHURT TORTE
Serves 6–8

1 ◆ For the base, mix together the almonds, sugar, breadcrumbs and baking powder in a bowl. Whisk the egg whites and fold into the dry ingredients.
2 ◆ Turn the mixture into a lightly greased 20cm/8in round cake tin with removable base, and smooth the surface. Cook in a preheated oven at 180°C/gas 4 for 30-35 min until firm and lightly browned. Leave to cool in the dish.
3 ◆ For the topping, sprinkle the gelatin on to the wine and leave to soak for a few minutes. Heat gently in a small pan until hot then stir until dissolved.
4 ◆ Gently stir the cream with the yoghurt to blend and fold in the gelatin.
5 ◆ Whisk the egg whites with the caster sugar until holding soft peaks and fold into the cream and yoghurt mixture. Fold in half the grapes and turn the mixture into the tin. Chill for 2 hr until set.
6 ◆ Carefully remove the torte from the dish on to a serving plate and arrange concentric circles of the remaining grapes on the top of the mousse.

for the almond base:
100g/4oz ground almonds
90g/3¹/2oz caster sugar
50g/2oz fresh breadcrumbs
4ml/³/4tsp baking powder
3 egg whites

for the mousse:
1 sachet powdered gelatin
75ml/3fl oz/¹/3 cup dry white wine
150ml/¹/4pt/²/3 cup double cream (heavy cream), lightly whipped
150ml/¹/4pt/²/3 cup natural yoghurt
2 egg whites
30ml/2tbsp/3tbsp caster sugar
225g/8oz seedless white grapes

LIGHT LEMON SYLLABUB
Serves 4

1 ◆ Mix together the lemon juice and rind with the honey and brandy in a bowl.
2 ◆ Mash the soft cheese with a wooden spoon, beat lightly then blend with the juices, honey and brandy.
3 ◆ Whip the cream until stiff and gently fold into the cheese mixture.
4 ◆ Pour into four glass-stemmed dishes or wine glasses and chill.
5 ◆ Sprinkle with toasted flaked almonds and decorate with lemon curls. Serve with ratafia or sponge biscuits.

30ml/2tbsp/3tbsp lemon juice
¹/2 lemon, grated rind
15ml/1tbsp clear honey (thin honey)
15-30ml/1-2tbsp/1-3tbsp brandy
175g/6oz low fat soft cheese
90ml/6tbsp/8tbsp whipping cream
toasted flaked almonds and lemon curls to decorate
ratafia or sponge biscuits for serving

RASPBERRY SYLLABUB
Serves 4

1 • Purée the raspberries in a food processor or blender and rub through a sieve if preferred to remove the pips.
2 • Stir the lemon juice and rind into the purée then stir in the sugar and double cream (heavy cream).
3 • Whisk the mixture until soft peaks form and turn into individual dishes or dessert glasses. Serve with extra fresh raspberries if liked.

175g/6oz raspberries
juice 1/2 lemon
grated rind of 1 lemon
150g/5oz caster sugar
275ml/1/2pt/11/4 cups double cream (heavy cream)
fresh raspberries for serving

SOUTH SEAS PARFAIT
Serves 4

You can use almost any exotic fruit to make this sweet delight but as it is finished and assembled at the last minute, it really is best if you use an electric mixer to do the whisking.

1 • Halve the pawpaw and scoop out the seeds or cut the mango in halves around the stone. Remove the flesh from the skin and roughly chop.
2 • Place the flesh into a pan with the lime or lemon juice and water. Heat gently and simmer for 8-10 min or until softened, then mash to a pulp with a fork and stir in half the liqueur.
3 • Whisk the egg yolks with the caster sugar and the rest of the liqueur over a bowl of hot water until it becomes pale in colour and very thick and frothy, when it will have trebled in volume.
4 • Spoon layers of the fruit and whisked egg yolk mixture into dessert glasses and sprinkle with the desiccated coconut.
5 • Decorate each glass with a slice of lime if liked and serve while still slightly warm with crisp dessert biscuits.

1 fresh ripe pawpaw or mango, about 350-450g/12-16oz
juice 1 small lime
45ml/3tbsp/4tbsp water
3 egg yolks
75g/3oz caster sugar
45ml/3tbsp/4tbsp Malibu, rum or brandy
30ml/2tbsp/3tbsp desiccated coconut, toasted
4 slices lime for decoration, optional
crisp dessert biscuits such as langues de chat for serving (page 108)

(*From left*) Raspberry Syllabub; South Sea Parfait; Light Lemon Syllabub

INDIVIDUAL HONEY BREAD PUDDINGS
Serves 4

4-5 thick slices white bread,
  crusts removed
butter for spreading
3 eggs
30-45ml/2-3tbsp/3-4tbsp clear
  honey (thin honey)
200ml/7fl oz/1 cup milk
single cream (light cream) for
  serving

*Golden syrup (light corn syrup) makes a good
alternative to the honey.*

1 ◆ Preheat the oven to 180°C/gas 4.
2 ◆ Toast one side of the bread under a hot grill and butter the toasted side. Cut into small cubes and arrange into four 150ml/ ¼pt ramekin dishes.
3 ◆ Whisk together the eggs with about 15-25ml/1-1½tbsp/1-2 tbsp of the honey to taste and the milk, and pour over the bread.
4 ◆ Place the dishes on to a baking tray for easy handling and bake for 20-30 min until puffed and golden.
5 ◆ Drizzle each pudding with a little more honey and serve straight away with some single cream (light cream).

MINT CHOCOLATE SOUFFLÉS
Serves 6

butter for greasing
150ml/¹/4pt/²/3 cup milk
12 After Eight mints
25g/1oz butter
20g/³/4oz plain flour (all-
  purpose flour)
25g/1oz caster sugar
3 eggs, separated

1 ◆ Lightly butter 6 ramekin dishes. Preheat the oven to 190°C/gas 5.
2 ◆ Heat the milk in a pan with the mints until melted and blended. Set to one side.
3 ◆ In another pan, melt the 25g/1oz butter, stir in the flour and cook for 1 min, stirring all the time. Off the heat, gradually stir in the milk until well blended.
4 ◆ Return to the heat and stirring all the time, bring to the boil. Cook for 1 min then allow to cool slightly before beating in the sugar and egg yolks.
5 ◆ Whisk the egg whites until stiff (but not dry) and gently fold into the sauce. Spoon into the prepared dishes and place on a baking tray for easy handling.
6 ◆ Bake for 15-20 min until risen and set. Serve straight away.

PEACH AND ALMOND TRIFLE
Serves 6–8

1 • Crumble the trifle sponges and macaroons together over the base of a dish. Dot with apricot jam.
2 • Sprinkle over the brandy or wine and any juice from the prepared peaches.
3 • Layer the fruit, pour over the custard and chill.
4 • Decorate with grated chocolate, rosettes of cream and toasted flaked almonds.

225g/8oz trifle sponges and macaroons, mixed
25g/1oz apricot jam
75ml/3fl oz/¹/3 cup brandy or white wine or a combination
450-675g/1-1¹/2lb peaches, skinned and sliced
550ml/1pt/2¹/2 cups custard chocolate, grated
150ml/¹/4pt/²/3 cup double cream (heavy cream)
25-50g/1-2oz flaked almonds, toasted

ELDERFLOWER AND RHUBARB SNOW
Serves 2

1 • Place the elderflowers, rhubarb, half the orange juice and the sugar into a pan and heat gently until the rhubarb begins to soften and the sugar is dissolved. Cover and simmer for 6-8 min until tender then leave to cool.
2 • Meanwhile, place the remaining orange juice into a small saucepan and sprinkle with the gelatin. Leave to soak for a few minutes then heat very gently until the gelatin has dissolved.
3 • Remove and discard the elderflowers from the fruit then purée the rhubarb in a food processor or blender. Stir in the gelatin and chill until beginning to set.
4 • Whisk the egg white with the cream of tartar until soft peaks form then fold into the rhubarb purée. Transfer into individual serving dishes or glasses and chill until set.
5 • Place the chilled dishes on to plates decorated with elderflowers. Serve with crisp dessert biscuits.

2 large sprigs elderflowers
175-225g/6-8oz young rhubarb, cut into 2.5cm/1in pieces
60ml/4tbsp/5tbsp freshly squeezed orange juice
40g/1¹/2oz sugar to taste
10ml/2tsp gelatin
1 large egg white
pinch cream tartar
elderflowers for decoration, optional
crisp dessert biscuits for serving (page 108)

CHAMPAGNE MELON WITH STRAWBERRIES
Serves 4–6

225g/8oz small strawberries
1 orange-fleshed melon such as
  Charantais or Cantaloupe
1 green-fleshed melon such as
  Ogen or Galia
15-30ml/1-2tbsp/1-3tbsp icing
  sugar (confectioner's sugar)
15-30ml/1-2tbsp/1-3tbsp brandy
225ml/8fl oz/1 cup champagne
  (or sparkling wine)
few drops cassis, optional
mint leaves for decoration

1 • Hull, wash and dry the strawberries. If large, cut them in halves.
2 • Halve the melons, remove the seeds and cut out the flesh with a melon baller or cut into neat cubes.
3 • Place the fruit into a serving dish, sprinkle with the icing sugar (confectioner's sugar) and brandy. Cover and leave to marinate in the refrigerator until required.
4 • Meanwhile, chill the champagne and when ready to serve pour it over the fruit with a few drops of cassis if liked to give a pink tinge to the champagne.

CHERRIES IN CLARET
Serves 6

675g/1¹/₂lb fresh cherries, or
  pitted frozen cherries
1 bottle claret
sugar to taste
pinch cinnamon
45ml/3tbsp/4tbsp redcurrant
  jelly
4-6 dessertspoons of thick cream
  for serving, optional

1 • Wash, stone and dry fresh cherries, defrost frozen ones.
2 • Pour the claret into a large saucepan, add the sugar and cinnamon. Gently bring to the boil, stirring to dissolve the sugar, then simmer for 4-5 min.
3 • Add the cherries to the pan and continue to simmer for 3-4 min. Remove the cherries from the pan with a slotted spoon to a serving dish.
4 • Bring the wine to the boil and simmer vigorously to reduce the quantity by about one-third. Stir in the redcurrant jelly until dissolved.
5 • Add the syrup to the cherries and allow to cool then chill. Serve in individual dishes with a spoonful of cream swirled in the centre if liked.

(*From top*) Champagne Melon with Strawberries; Cherries in Claret;
Elderflower and Rhubarb Snow

GRAPEFRUIT IN BRANDY
Serves 4

3 large grapefruit
50-75g/2-3oz demerara sugar
  (brown sugar)
150ml/¹/4pt/²/3 cup water
5ml/1tsp cinnamon
45ml/3tbsp/4 tbsp brandy
strawberry leaves and flowers for
  garnish, optional

Served on their own, this dessert is very refreshing after a rich meal.

1 ‣ Peel the grapefruits and remove all the pith. Carefully take out the centre cores with a skewer. Cut the fruit into 12mm/½in slices.
2 ‣ Add the sugar to taste to the water with the cinnamon in a saucepan. Heat gently, stirring to dissolve the sugar. Bring to the boil then simmer for 2 min.
3 ‣ Add the grapefruit to the pan and continue to simmer for 2-3 min, turning the slices over in the syrup half-way through.
4 ‣ Using a draining spoon, transfer the fruit to a serving dish. Boil up the juices for 2 min.
5 ‣ Mix 45-60ml/3-4tbsp/4-5tbsp of the syrup with the brandy and pour over the grapefruit. Serve warm or chilled on their own or with the garnish.

PEACH AND RASPBERRY PLATTER
Serves 4

4 peaches (or 450g/1lb canned
  peaches in natural syrup)
boiling water
225g/8oz raspberries
honey, sugar or concentrated
  apple juice to taste
150ml/¹/4pt/²/3 cup fromage
  frais or Greek natural yoghurt
a little water
a few pistachios for decoration,
  optional

1 ‣ Place the fresh peaches in a large bowl and pour over boiling water to cover. Leave to stand for a few minutes then drain and carefully peel off the skins. Cut into halves and remove the stones then slice the flesh into neat thin slices. (If using canned peaches, drain and slice thinly.)
2 ‣ Purée the raspberries in a food processor or blender until smooth then add a little honey, sugar or concentrated apple juice to taste. Rub through a sieve to remove pips if preferred.
3 ‣ Mix the fromage frais or yoghurt with a little water to thin slightly and arrange alternate spoonsful of raspberry purée and fromage frais or yoghurt on 4 individual serving plates.
4 ‣ Swirl or marble the two colours together with a fork then carefully arrange the sliced peaches on the top. Decorate with a few pistachios if liked.

LIME SYLLABUB WITH STRAWBERRIES
Serves 6

Although this recipe uses strawberries, any dessert fruit can be served with the lime syllabub cream.

350g/12oz prepared dessert fruit, eg strawberries
2 limes, grated rind and juice
100ml/4fl oz/¹/2 cup medium white wine
50g/2oz caster sugar
275ml/¹/2pt/1¹/4 cups double cream (heavy cream)
150ml/¹/4pt/²/3 cup Greek natural yoghurt

1 • Reserve six strawberries for decoration, then slice the rest and divide between six dishes.
2 • Mix the lime rind and juice with the wine and sugar. Stir until the sugar is dissolved.
3 • Whip the double cream (heavy cream) until beginning to hold its shape, then gradually whisk in the wine mixture until the cream thickens slightly. Whisk in the yoghurt.
4 • Spoon the cream over the fruit and chill for 10 min before serving garnished with the reserved fruit.

Note: If preferred for an alternative serving arrangement, the cream may be poured onto plates and the fruit arranged attractively on top.

GRAPE AND WINE JELLIES
Serves 4

30ml/2tbsp/3tbsp cold water
10ml/2tsp powdered gelatin
¹/2 bottle sweet white wine, eg Sauternes
10ml/2tsp caster sugar
225g/¹/2lb green or black grapes, or a mixture, halved and deseeded
single cream (light cream) and dessert biscuits for serving

1 • Measure the cold water into a small bowl and sprinkle on the gelatin. Leave to soak for 10 min then stand the bowl in a pan of simmering water to dissolve the gelatin.
2 • Meanwhile, gently heat 60-75ml/4-5tbsp/5-6tbsp of the wine with the sugar, stirring until the sugar is dissolved. Add to the rest of the wine with the dissolved gelatin. Cool, then chill until just setting.
3 • When the jelly is almost set, stir in the prepared grapes then quickly pour into individual serving dishes. Chill until set and serve with cream and crisp dessert biscuits.

(*Overleaf, from top*) Grapefruit in Brandy; Peach and Raspberry Platter

APPLE FRUIT COMPÔTE
Serves 4–6

650-825ml/1¼-1½pt/3-3¾
 cups apple juice
100-175g/4-6oz each ready-to-
 eat prunes, apricots and figs
30-45ml/2-3tbsp/3-4tbsp
 Calvados, optional
25g/1oz walnuts, chopped
curls of orange or lemon rind for
 decoration, optional

1 ♦ Place the apple juice and fruit into a large saucepan. Bring to the boil, cover and simmer for 20-25 min until the fruits are tender.
2 ♦ Stir in the Calvados (or brandy) if liked and leave to cool.
3 ♦ Sprinkle with the chopped walnuts and serve warm or cold decorated with curls of orange or lemon rind.

TROPICAL FRUIT SALAD
Serves 2

1 lemon
25-40g/1½-2tbsp/2-3tbsp
 caster sugar, to taste
60ml/4tbsp/5tbsp water
6 cloves
6-8 kumquats
2 kiwi fruits
4-5 fresh dates
10ml/2tsp orange flower water
15-30ml/1-2tbsp/1-3tbsp
 Malibu liqueur, optional
yoghurt, cream or ice-cream for
 serving

1 ♦ Thinly pare the rind from the lemon with a potato peeler then squeeze the juice and set it to one side.
2 ♦ Place the lemon rind in a small saucepan with the sugar, water and cloves. Bring to the boil, stirring, until the sugar has dissolved. Remove from the heat and leave until cold.
3 ♦ Slice the kumquats into halves lengthways, peel and slice the kiwi fruit and halve and stone the dates. Place the fruit in a serving dish.
4 ♦ Strain the syrup into a jug, stir in the reserved lemon juice with the orange flower water and the Malibu if liked.
5 ♦ Pour over the fruit and chill until required. Serve with yoghurt, cream or ice-cream.

(*Previous page, from top*) Apple Fruit Compôte; Tropical Salad; Hot Blackberry Fool

HOT BLACKBERRY FOOL
Serves 4

This frothy desserts needs last minute assembling as it needs to be served immediately, while still warm.

1 • Place the blackberries in a pan with the spirit, water and 25g/1oz of the icing sugar (confectioner's sugar). Heat gently and simmer for 6-8 min until just tender. Break up the blackberries slightly with a fork.
2 • Meanwhile, whisk the egg whites until stiff then gradually whisk in the remaining icing sugar (confectioner's sugar).
3 • Gently fold the blackberries into the meringue and spoon into serving glasses. Serve straight away.

225g/8oz blackberries
30ml/2tbsp/3tbsp white rum, gin or kirsch
15ml/1tbsp water
100g/4oz icing sugar (confectioner's sugar)
2 egg whites

CHOCOLATE FRUIT
Serves 2

1 • Wash and dry fruits such as strawberries and grapes, retaining the stalks where appropriate. Cut pineapple into segments, make melon balls and dry these fruits thoroughly with kitchen paper (paper towels). Spear the pieces of fruit on to cocktail sticks for easy handling.
2 • Meanwhile, break up the chocolate into a bowl and heat gently over a pan of hot water until melted. Stir well.
3 • Dip the fruits into the chocolate and leave to harden. Try to do this without laying the pieces on to a surface by impaling the other end of the cocktail sticks into a large potato.
4 • Serve the chocolate fruit with thick or whipped cream if liked.

2 portions fresh, mixed fruit such as strawberries, grapes, pineapple, melon
50-75g/2-3oz plain dessert chocolate (bitter chocolate)
30-60ml/2-4tbsp/3-5tbsp thick or whipped cream flavoured with a little kirsch if liked for serving

CHOCOLATE AND FRUIT FONDUE

1 • Follow the ingredients for chocolate fruit above.
2 • Place the prepared bite-size fruits into serving bowls and sprinkle with a little kirsch.
3 • Stir the cream into the melted chocolate with a knob of butter.
4 • Keeping the chocolate mixture warm, serve the fruits with fondue forks or cocktail sticks to spear the fruits for dipping into the chocolate.

CHOCOLATE AND ALMOND TERRINE WITH COFFEE CREAM
Serves 8-12

225g/8oz plain chocolate (bitter chocolate), melted
50ml/2fl oz/1/4 cup dark rum or brandy
225g/8oz unsalted butter, softened
75g/3oz caster sugar
3 eggs, size 1 (large), separated
175g/6oz ground almonds
100g/4oz rich tea biscuits, crushed into small pieces
almond or walnut oil for brushing
275ml/1/2pt/1 1/4 cups whipping cream
10ml/2tsp instant coffee dissolved in 50ml/2fl oz/1/4 cup boiling water and chilled

This calorific chocolate dessert can be made a day or two ahead of time and is best served after a not too rich meal.

1 ◆ Mix together the melted chocolate and rum or brandy and keep warm.
2 ◆ Beat the butter and sugar until soft and creamy, beat in the egg yolks, then combine with the almonds and chocolate mixture and mix well.
3 ◆ Whisk the egg whites until very stiff and gently fold into the almond mixture with the biscuits.
4 ◆ Turn the mixture into an oiled 900g/2lb loaf tin and smooth the top. Cover and freeze for 2 hr then remove and refrigerate for at least 6 hr or until required.
5 ◆ When ready to serve, whip the cream until holding soft peaks and add the chilled coffee. The mixture will be soft.
6 ◆ Loosen the terrine with a knife dipped in hot water and invert on to a chilled serving platter. Serve cut into slices and with spoonsful of coffee cream.

SUMMER FRUIT BOWL WITH COCONUT
Serves 6–8

1 ripe melon such as Galia
1 or 2 ripe papayas
485g/1lb 1oz can lychees
juice of 1 lime or 30ml/2tbsp/3tbsp orange juice
25-40g/1-1 1/2oz large coconut flakes

1 ◆ Halve the melon and papayas, discard the seeds, then cut the flesh into large chunks or use a melon baller. Arrange in a serving bowl.
2 ◆ Drain the juice from the lychees into the bowl, cut the lychees into halves and stir into the bowl with the lime juice.
3 ◆ Cover the bowl and chill. Toast the coconut and sprinkle over the fruit before serving.

(From top) Chocolate Fruit; Chocolate and Almond Terrine with Coffee Cream

RASPBERRIES IN RASPBERRY VINEGAR
Serves 6

675g/1¹/2lb raspberries
175g/6oz caster sugar
275ml/¹/2pt/1¹/4 cups water
30ml/2tbsp/3tbsp raspberry
  vinegar
borage flowers for decoration,
  optional
cream for serving

1 • Wash the raspberries and place in a large serving dish.
2 • Dissolve the sugar in 200ml/7fl oz/1 cup of the water over a gentle heat, without stirring.
3 • Bring to the boil and boil until the syrup is a light caramel colour. Remove from the heat and add the rest of the water and the raspberry vinegar. Heat again if necessary to dissolve any hardened caramel.
4 • Pour the syrup over the raspberries and leave to cool then chill. Serve decorated with flowers of borage if liked, and hand the cream separately.

CREAMED RICE COMPÔTE
Serves 4

425g/15oz can creamed rice
150g/¹/4pt/²/3 cup Greek
  natural yoghurt
1 lemon, grated rind and
  30ml/2tbsp/3tbsp juice
12 ratafias
90ml/6tbsp/8tbsp redcurrant
  jelly

1 • Mix together the creamed rice, yoghurt and grated lemon rind.
2 • Divide the mixture between four 150ml/¹/4pt ramekin dishes and arrange the ratafias on the top.
3 • In a small pan, mix the lemon juice and redcurrant jelly and heat gently, stirring, until smooth. Allow the mixture to boil for a minute to reduce the quantity slightly.
4 • Drizzle the redcurrant glaze over the compôtes and chill before serving.

PEARS IN RED WINE
Serves 6

150g/5oz sugar
150ml/¹/4pt/²/3 cup water
150ml/¹/4pt/²/3 cup red wine
2.5cm/1in piece of cinnamon stick
6 dessert pears, peeled, stalks
  remaining
10ml/2tsp arrowroot, mixed with
  a little water
whipped cream for serving

1 • Place sugar, water, wine and cinnamon in a pan. Heat gently until sugar is dissolved. Bring to boil, boil for 5 min.
2 • Add the pears, cover and simmer for 20-30 min or just tender.
3 • Remove cinnamon stick. Transfer the pears to serving dish.
4 • Add arrowroot mixture to the syrup. Bring to boil, stirring. Simmer for 1 min until clear, then cool slightly.
5 • Spoon the syrup over pears, chill. Serve with whipped cream.

ORANGES IN CARAMEL
Serves 4

1 ◆ Pare and finely shred the rind from one orange. Blanch, drain and dry.
2 ◆ Peel the other oranges and remove pith. Cut into thin slices, hold together with cocktail sticks. Arrange in individual dishes and sprinkle with the liqueur.
3 ◆ Heat sugar and cold water gently until sugar dissolves. Bring to the boil. Boil steadily (do not stir) until the mixture turns a rich brown colour.
4 ◆ Carefully add hot water and stir until caramel has melted, heat again if necessary. Leave to cool.
5 ◆ Pour the caramel over the oranges, decorate with shredded rind. Chill.
6 ◆ Serve with crisp dessert biscuits.

4 large or 8 small oranges
30ml/2tbsp/3tbsp Grand Marnier or Cointreau
225g/8oz sugar
150ml/¹/4pt/²/3 cup cold water
150ml/¹/4pt/²/3 cup hot water
dessert biscuits for serving

CRANACHAN
Serves 4

A delicious mixture of textures. Vary the fruit according to the season.

1 ◆ Preheat the oven to 180°C/gas 4.
2 ◆ Save 4 hazelnuts for decoration, coarsely grind the rest in a food processor or blender.
3 ◆ Mix the ground hazelnuts with the oatmeal and place on a baking tray with the 4 reserved whole hazelnuts. Toast in the hot oven for 10-15 min until golden. Leave to cool.
4 ◆ Layer the oatmeal and hazelnut mixture with the fruits and yoghurt or cream. Finish with a layer of yoghurt or cream.
5 ◆ Decorate with raspberries or strawberries and reserved whole hazelnuts.

75g/3oz hazelnuts
75g/3oz medium oatmeal
150g/¹/4pt/²/3 cup Greek natural yoghurt or thick cream
225g/8oz black grapes, halved and deseeded
225g/8oz white grapes, halved and deseeded or strawberries, sliced
few whole raspberries or small strawberries for decoration

SOURED CREAM BRÛLÉE WITH RASPBERRIES
Serves 3–4

350g/12oz raspberries (thawed if frozen)
15-25ml/1-1¹/₂tbsp/1-2tbsp dry white wine or sherry
150-175ml/5-6fl oz/²/₃-³/₄ cup soured cream (sour cream)
100g/4oz soft brown sugar

1 ◆ Reserve a few raspberries for decoration. Divide the rest between 3-4 heatproof ramekin dishes.
2 ◆ Sprinkle the fruit with the wine or sherry and top with the soured cream. Chill in the refrigerator.
3 ◆ Make a caramel with the brown sugar and 60ml/4tbsp/5tbsp water and carefully pour over the soured cream. Alternatively, sprinkle the soured cream with the sugar and brown under a hot grill to caramalise the sugar.
4 ◆ Serve warm or chilled, sprinkled with a little brown sugar and decorated with the reserved raspberries.

STRAWBERRIES FLAMBÉS
Serves 4–6

100g/4oz soft light brown sugar
150ml/¹/₄pt/²/₃ cup orange juice
15ml/1tbsp lemon juice
30ml/2tbsp/3tbsp finely grated orange rind
15ml/1tbsp finely grated lemon rind
675g/1¹/₂lb strawberries, hulled, washed and dried
45-60ml/3-4tbsp/4-5tbsp brandy
fine curls of orange or lemon peel to garnish
ice-cream to serve

1 ◆ Heat the sugar, juices and grated rind gently in a pan, stirring to dissolve the sugar.
2 ◆ Bring the syrup to the boil then remove from the heat.
3 ◆ Add the strawberries to the pan and turn them over so they are coated with the syrup.
4 ◆ Heat the brandy until hot, pour over the strawberries and ignite.
5 ◆ When the flames have gone, stir gently and serve with ice-cream.

(*From top*) Strawberries Flambés; Soured Cream Brûlée with Raspberries; Cranachan

CHOCOLATE CHEESECAKE
Serves 6–8

50g/2oz butter, melted
150ml/5oz digestive biscuits
  (graham crackers) finely crushed
2.5ml/1tsp ground cinnamon
225g/8oz cream cheese
75g/3oz sugar
2 eggs, separated
175g/6oz plain chocolate, melted
275ml/¹/2pt/1¹/4 cups double
  cream (heavy cream), lightly
  whipped
grated chocolate

1 ♦ Mix butter, biscuit crumbs and cinnamon together. Line the base and sides of a 23cm/9in flan ring with crumb mixture. Place in refrigerator to harden.
2 ♦ Blend the cheese, sugar and egg yolks together. Mix in the chocolate. Fold in half the cream.
3 ♦ Whisk egg whites until stiff, fold into the mixture. Spoon into the crumb base. Leave to set in the refrigerator.
4 ♦ Decorate with rosettes of cream and grated chocolate.

HONEY AND ALMOND BAKED APPLES
Serves 4

4 medium/large cooking apples
40g/1¹/2oz butter
50g/2oz soft brown sugar
25g/1oz sultanas
30ml/2tbsp/3tbsp chopped
  almonds
30ml/2tbsp/3tbsp water
15ml/1tbsp/2tbsp lemon juice
30ml/2tbsp/3tbsp clear honey

1 ♦ Core the apples, but do not peel. Score them around the middle and place in a suitable size baking dish.
2 ♦ Mix together the butter, sugar, sultanas and nuts. Fill the centre of each apple with the mixture.
3 ♦ Warm and blend the water, lemon juice and honey together and spoon over the apples.
4 ♦ Bake until the apples are soft, but still retain their shape, 35-45 min at 180°C/gas 4.
5 ♦ Serve warm with cream.

HIGHLAND SYLLABUB
Serves 4–6

30ml/2tbsp/3tbsp clear honey
45ml/3tbsp/4tbsp whisky
15ml/1tbsp/2tbsp lemon juice
275ml/¹/2pt/1¹/4 cups double
  cream (heavy cream)
15-25ml/1-1¹/2tbsp/1¹/2-2tbsp
  fine oatmeal

1 ♦ Place the honey into a saucepan and heat gently until just warm and runny.
2 ♦ Beat in the whisky and lemon juice until well blended. Add the double cream (heavy cream) and whisk the ingredients together until light and fluffy and the mixture has thickened.
3 ♦ Spoon the mixture into 4-6 individual serving glasses and chill for 2-3 hrs.
4 ♦ Toast the oats under a hot grill. Leave to cool then sprinkle over the top of the syllabubs before serving.

GOLDEN BAKED APPLE SLICES
Serves 4

1 ▸ Preheat the oven to 200°C/gas 6. Peel, quarter and core the apples then cut into thick slices measuring about 12mm/½in at the outside edge.
2 ▸ Place the syrup or honey, cinnamon, lemon juice and butter into a saucepan and heat gently until melted. Toss the apple slices into the melted mixture.
3 ▸ Arrange overlapping apple slices in a shallow dish – in rows if an oblong dish or in circles if a round one – and pour over the remaining syrup mixture.
4 ▸ Bake for 30-40 min, basting the apples with the juices every 10 min. The apples should be tender but still holding shape and light golden brown when done.
5 ▸ If the juices have not thickened at the end of the cooking time, drain them into a saucepan and boil until reduced to a thick syrup, then pour over the apples.

6 dessert apples
30-45ml/2-3tbsp/3-4tbsp golden syrup or clear honey (light corn syrup or thin honey)
2.5ml/¹/₂tsp ground cinnamon
15ml/1tbsp lemon juice
25-50g/1-2oz butter, melted cream, natural yoghurt or ice-cream for serving

CREAM CHEESE STRUDEL
Serves 2

This recipe is to make two individual strudels, but you could make and cook one large one if preferred.

1 ▸ Place the sultanas and lemon juice in a small pan, heat gently and simmer for 1½-2 min. Leave to cool. Preheat the oven to 180°C/gas 4.
2 ▸ Blend the cream cheese, lemon rind, butter, sugar, vanilla essence (vanilla extract) and bread or cake crumbs together. Add a few drops of milk if necessary to make a soft consistency. Drain the sultanas and add to the mixture.
3 ▸ Cut the filo pastry into two and with the short edges facing, lay out the sheets and brush with oil. Place the cream cheese mixture in a sausage shape 2.5cm/1in from the facing (short) edge, leaving 4-5cm/1½-2in at each side.
4 ▸ Fold the short edge and sides over and then roll up. Place on to a baking sheet, brush the strudels with melted butter and bake for 15-20 min or until golden brown.

25g/1oz sultanas
1 lemon, juice and grated rind
100g/4oz cream cheese
15ml/1tbsp caster sugar
few drops vanilla essence (vanilla extract)
25g/1oz fresh bread or cake crumbs
few drops milk if necessary
1 sheet filo pastry, approximately 60x40cm/24x18in
10ml/2tsp oil
melted butter for brushing
icing sugar (confectioner's sugar) for dredging

Recipe Index

Numbers in italics indicate photographs

(From top) Cream Cheese Strudel; Golden Baked Apple Slices